THE SUBJECTIVE VIEW

THE SUBJECTIVE VIEW

Secondary Qualities and Indexical Thoughts

COLIN McGINN

CLARENDON PRESS · OXFORD
1983

Oxford University Press, Walton Street, Oxford

London Glasgow New York Toronto
Delhi Bombay Calcutta Madras Karachi
Kuala Lumpur Singapore Hong Kong Tokyo
Nairobi Dar es Salaam Cape Town
Melbourne Auckland

and associated companies in
Beirut Berlin Ibadan Mexico City Nicosia

OXFORD *is a trade mark of Oxford University Press*

Published in the United States
by Oxford University Press, New York

© *Colin McGinn 1983*

British Library Cataloguing in Publication Data

McGinn, Colin
    The subjective view: secondary qualities and
    indexical thoughts.
    1. Idealism
    I. Title
    141   B823

    ISBN 0-19-824696-X
    ISBN 0-19-824695-1 Pbk

Library of Congress Cataloging in Publication Data

McGinn, Colin, 1950–
    The subjective view.

    Bibliography: p.
    Includes index.
    1. Subjectivity.   2. Objectivity.   I. Title.
BD222.M4   1983   121'.4   83–4025
ISBN 0-19-824696-X
ISBN 0-19-824695-1 (pbk.)

Typeset by Joshua Associates, Oxford
Printed in Great Britain
at the University Press, Oxford
by Eric Buckley
Printer to the University

Preface

This monograph is occupied with the relationship between the world as it is independently of the mind and the world as it is presented to the mind. I put forward the thesis that it is a necessary truth that the world is not presented to us just as it is in itself. This thesis raises two questions: how, if the thesis is correct, do we come by an objective conception of the world? and why is it that the world must be presented to us in a subjective way? These questions, and allied matters, are approached by considering the perception of secondary qualities and the having of indexical thoughts.

I did not initially intend that this work would finish up in book form, but I found that I had too much material to fit into a single article and the material was too interconnected to be made into several articles. The style of the book is thus like that of an extended article: unselfcontained, exploratory, inconclusive. I hope, at least, that my readers will be convinced of the genuineness and difficulty of the questions I raise, and that they may be stimulated to make progress on the issues where my own efforts have met with less than total success.

I have discussed the ideas of the book with many people and have been helped in seeing the issues more clearly. In view of the slightness of the result, it would be faintly absurd to mention all these people, but I must acknowledge in particular Anita Avramides, Malcolm Budd, Ian McFetridge, Jim Hopkins and Arnold Zuboff. Katherine Backhouse was kind enough to do the typing, and University College gave me a sabbatical term (Autumn 1981) during which the book was written.

Colin McGinn
2 July 1982

Contents

1
Introduction

There are various ways in which the mind represents the world. It is legitimate to enquire, of any way in which the world is mentally represented, whether that way is subjective or objective in nature: that is, to enquire whether the world is so represented because of the specific constitution of the representing mind or because the world as it is independently of the mind contains a feature which demands representation. Which aspects of our view of reality have their source in our subjective make-up and which reflect reality as it is in itself? This question lies at the intersection of metaphysics and the philosophy of mind; to answer it would be to learn something both about how the mind is (or must be) and about how the world is objectively constituted. Once we have a demarcation of subjective and objective ways of representing the world, we can ask the further question of what is distinctive of each and precisely how they are related. Are there any general principles governing subjective and objective modes of representation? Is one more basic than the other? Is either eliminable in some way? Does one possess greater verisimilitude than the other? These are familiar-sounding questions, though questions on which it is hard to get a firm grip: one feels that they are perfectly proper, but the generality and airiness of their formulation hampers any sharp-edged investigation of the issues raised. What is wanted is the identification of some specific aspect of our view of the world which permits a more precise formulation of issues. That is what I attempt in this essay. My aim is to make these abstract questions concrete and tractable by considering two types of subjective representation in some detail, contrasting them with more objective ways in which the world is represented.

The types of subjective representation in question are indexical thought and experience of secondary qualities; I shall be taking these to be instances of a subjective view of the world, in a sense I will try to make precise. Their distinctive features will be elucidated and contrasted with representations involving non-indexical thoughts and perception of primary qualities. The question of their eliminability will be discussed, and some suggestions made about how the subjective view they exemplify relates to an objective conception of the world. My procedure will be to pursue these questions by considering indexicals and secondary qualities in parallel, developing certain analogies between them. It is not my primary concern to urge the interest of the analogies as such, though I think them more striking than might initially be suspected; it is rather to arrive at an account of each which will shed some light on the general issues about subjectivity with which I am concerned. But it proves convenient and heuristically helpful to investigate the two topics in tandem, as I hope will become apparent. Parallel questions arise about indexicals and secondary qualities, and results derived in one area can provide clues to the correct account of the other. I should also say that, though my motivating concern is with the bearing of these two topics upon the general question of the nature of subjective and objective representations, they raise interesting questions in their own right, and I shall spend a good deal of time endeavouring to give answers to these questions. I shall begin by explaining the sense in which secondary qualities are subjective and spelling out some implications of their subjectivity; then I shall address the question in what sense indexicals are subjective, noting certain analogies with secondary qualities. I will not supply a full defence of these theses about secondary qualities and indexicals, since others have argued convincingly for the key points and I do not anticipate much disagreement with the position I adopt; what follows in chapter 2 is intended merely to lay out the background for later developments and to highlight certain consequences of (fairly) standard views of these matters.

2
Some Preliminary Theses

According to the Lockean tradition, secondary qualities are defined as those whose instantiation in an object consists in a power or disposition of the object to produce sensory experiences in perceivers of a certain phenomenological character; whereas primary qualities are said not to consist in such dispositions to produce experiences.[1] This is simply a stipulative definition of the distinction, leaving it open whether there are in fact any qualities of objects falling under either characterisation; it is thus a substantive question whether (say) colour is a secondary quality. The Lockean tradition then claims that we can assign familiar perceptible qualities of objects to one or other of the two categories: it claims that colours and tastes and sounds and felt qualities and smells belong to the category of secondary qualities, whereas shape and size and weight and motion belong to the category of primary qualities. These lists are not exhaustive, but they indicate the kinds of quality which are to count as secondary or primary in the defined sense. The idea is that we can recognise, of any given perceptible quality, into which category it falls, though we may not be able to supply any non-circular condition which determines whether any arbitrary quality is primary or secondary. For example, it is supposed that we can recognise that red is a secondary quality in the sense defined; for an object to be red is for it to present a certain kind of sensory appearance to perceivers. On the other hand, being cubical is recognised not to consist in such a disposition but in some intrinsic feature of the object. It is this general (and received) account of the

---

[1] See Locke, *An Essay Concerning Human Understanding, passim*; Reginald Jackson, 'Locke's Distinction Between Primary and Secondary Qualities'; W. C. Kneale, 'Sensation and the Physical World'; Jonathan Bennett, 'Primary and Secondary Qualities' (chap. IV of *Locke, Berkeley, Hume*).

distinction and its application that I propose to assume in what follows.

It is sometimes supposed that the dispositional thesis about (say) colour involves a circularity the exposure of which undermines any significant distinction between primary and secondary qualities. The circularity is supposed to be this: to specify which kinds of experience a red object is disposed to produce we need to *use* the word 'red' —but then the dispositional analysis of being red in terms of how things visually seem is circular. We need to use the word 'red' (i.e. invoke the concept of being red) because how a red object seems is precisely a matter of its looking *red*. Now I think it is true that there is no adequate specification of the relevant kinds of experience save by saying that the object looks red, but I do not think this should undermine our confidence in the primary/secondary distinction as we have defined it. Note, first, that the alleged circularity is of a peculiar kind, since it is not *generally* true that an object's looking Q entails that it is Q; this means that a claim of logical equivalence between 'is Q' and 'seems Q' will not be trivial, since not all values of 'Q' will sustain such an equivalence. Thus shape predicates do not sustain the equivalence while colour predicates do; and this asymmetry is quite independent of whether it is proper to hold that 'looks red' actually gives the meaning of 'red'. What we should claim is that being red *consists in* looking red; this is why the equivalence asserted by the dispositional thesis about red holds—though it is also true that 'looks red' is semantically complex, having 'red' as a semantically significant constituent. Indeed, even this non-definitional thesis is stronger than we strictly need to maintain the distinction from shape qualities; the bare assertion of logical or conceptual equivalence is enough to effect a distinction.[2]

---

[2] Thus we can affirm '$\Box(x$ is Q iff x (standardly) seems Q)' in case Q is a secondary quality; not so where Q is a primary quality. The force of the 'consists in' claim might be put by saying that, whereas an object looks square because it *is* square, an object is red because it *looks* red; and plainly this inversion does not imply the *semantic* priority of 'looks red' over 'red'. Such an inversion—with the

An analogy might help clarify the matter. Suppose we want to explain the distinction between attributive and predicative adjectives, i.e. the different ways in which they contribute to truth conditions. We compare, say, 'Jumbo is a tall elephant' with 'Jumbo is a ten ton elephant': and we suggest that the former is true if and only if Jumbo is taller than most elephants, whereas the latter cannot be said to be true if and only if Jumbo is more ten ton than most elephants. Now someone objects that we cannot draw the distinction in this way because the satisfaction condition for 'tall elephant' contains the word (or morpheme) 'tall' in a circular way—the condition is that Jumbo is *tall*er than most elephants. In response to such an objection we should, I think, agree that the proposed satisfaction condition does not explain the meaning of 'tall', but insist nevertheless (a) that the two are logically equivalent and (b) that the comparative form can be used to say what it *is* for the positive form to be satisfied—and these stand in contrast to predicative adjectives. (I do not say this is the correct view of attributive adjectives, only that it is coherent.)[3]

In the case of 'red' and 'looks red' it seems to me that the alleged circularity is just what we should expect, because we are explaining the instantiation of a quality in terms of the production of experiences with a certain intentional content—and such experiences necessarily consist in representing the world as having certain qualities. We might say that the 'circularity' arises, not because being red is inherently resistant to dispositional analysis, but rather because the analysans is inherently intentional: experiences are distinguished by their representational content, so naturally we shall need to use predicates of the external world in specifying them. The threat of circularity might tempt some to seek a non-intentional characterisation of the relevant kinds of

attendant use of the concept whose application conditions are being given within a psychological (oblique) context—is typical of accounts of properties which construe them as mind-dependent.

[3] For a discussion of attributive adjectives see John Wallace, 'Positive, Comparative, Superlative'.

experience, and failure in the search make them doubt the dispositional thesis; but I think that appreciating the source of the 'circularity' should dissuade us from undertaking the search and relieve any anxiety about the security of the dispositional thesis on account of its futility. The essential point is that, according to the dispositional thesis, the ultimate criterion for whether an object has a certain colour or taste (etc.) is how it looks and tastes to perceivers; whereas this is not how we think of qualities like shape and size. It does not compromise the claim that the *esse* of colour is *percipi* that the *percipi* can be specified only by using colour concepts. In future, then, I will allow myself to speak of *analysing* secondary qualities in terms of dispositions to produce sensory experiences, understanding by this the thesis that these experiential facts are *constitutive* of the presence of the quality in question.[4]

Let me now spell out some consequences of accepting the dispositional analysis of such qualities as colour and taste. An immediate consequence is that secondary qualities are subjective in the sense that experience enters into their analysis: to grasp the concept of red it is necessary to know what it is for something to look red, since this latter constitutes the satisfaction condition for an object's being red. In contrast, to grasp what it is for something to be square it is not constitutively necessary to know how square things look or feel, since what it *is* to be square does not involve any such relation to experience. But if grasping colour concepts requires knowledge of certain kinds of experience, and if (as is very plausible) this knowledge is available only to one who enjoys those kinds of experience, then grasp of colour concepts will depend upon the kind of acquaintance

---

[4] These points about secondary qualities show that it is not a good objection to a general phenomenalism that the content of the 'defining' experiences can only be specified in terms of the vocabulary to be 'defined': for the phenomenalist's thesis is (or ought to be) only that a disposition to enjoy experiences as of a certain external state of affairs is *constitutive of* (and so logically sufficient for) the obtaining of that state of affairs. This may be implausible, but there is nothing viciously circular about it.

with sensory experiences which we have only from the first-person perspective. In other words, colours are subjective in Thomas Nagel's sense: they are accessible only from a particular experiential point of view.[5] Primary qualities, since they are not similarly defined in relation to experience, are not subjective in this sense. A man born blind cannot appreciate what it is for something to be red because he lacks the subjective experiences analytic of being red. Secondary qualities are thus subjective in the way sensations are, even though they are ascribable to external things.

It is only slightly less obvious that the dispositional thesis implies the relativity of secondary qualities; for the question arises, to *which* perceiver or perceivers the red object is disposed to look red.[6] The same things can, of course, look different colours to different perceivers; so we need to ask whose experience fixes the correct application of the colour concepts. In practice there is a considerable measure of coincidence in the sensory appearances which things present to different perceivers, so that the constitutional relativity of colour ascriptions does not normally obtrude itself; but it is easy to describe cases in which this relativity is inescapable. Thus suppose a given range of objects looks systematically red to us and systematically green to Martians, and suppose our and their colour discriminations are equally fine.[7]

[5] See Nagel's 'What is it like to be a bat?' In this respect (as in others) it is helpful to consider Wittgenstein's analogy between red patches and pain patches: he says 'Let us imagine the following: The surfaces of the things around us (stones, plants, etc.) have patches and regions which produce pain in our skin when we touch them. (Perhaps through the chemical composition of these surfaces. But we need not know that.) In this case we should speak of pain-patches on the leaf of a particular plant just as at present we speak of red patches.' *Philosophical Investigations*, 312. Clearly, grasp of the property of (as we might say) 'paininess', as possessed by certain surfaces, would depend upon grasp of 'pain' as a predicate of sensations, and this requires knowledge of how pain feels.

[6] This relativity is well brought out by Bennett, op. cit., and by Bernard Williams, *Descartes*, pp. 241 ff.

[7] I should perhaps make it explicit that I am not supposing this difference of colour experience between Martians and us to be empirically undetectable: so the case does not require acceptance of the (alleged) possibility of spectrum inversion without behavioural repercussions. Note also that I have described the case in such a way as to exclude construing it in terms of a merely verbal difference—indeed the Martians could use the word 'red' to stand for the property of being green.

Then there will be no choosing between these groups of perceivers in respect of whose experience determines the colour
of the objects in question. Or suppose sugar goes from tasting
sweet to us to tasting bitter overnight, as a result of suitable
changes in our taste receptors. The dispositional thesis tells us
that sugar thereby ceases to be sweet and becomes bitter,
since what it is to have these qualities just consists in how
things taste. Secondary qualities resemble properties like being
poisonous or nourishing in this respect: plainly, these properties are relative to some implicit or explicit choice of creature
as that with respect to which a substance is declared poisonous
or nourishing. This relativity implies that there is no genuine
disagreement between us and the Martians when they call an
object green which we call red; for all these colour ascriptions
assert is that the object looks green to them and red to us. It
is thus entirely proper to speak of objects as red with respect
to perceiver x and green with respect to perceiver y. This is
not yet to say that colour predicates contain a suppressed
argument-place for a perceiver (or group of perceivers) in
logical form, so that they differ *semantically* from the syn-
tactically similar primary quality predicates; it is just to say
that what it is for a secondary quality to be instantiated is for a
certain relation to obtain between the object and some chosen
group of perceivers. It is this relativity that permits differences
in the perceived secondary qualities of things not to imply
genuine disagreement, whereas perceived differences of
primary qualities imply that at least one perceiver is in error.
This point of distinction between primary and secondary
qualities has the consequence that an inventory of the perceptible qualities of an object must be drawn up differently in
respect of the two categories: an object has as many colours
as there are different ways it (systematically) looks, but this
is not so for shape. There is thus a sense in which an object
has (or could have) many contrary colours simultaneously.[8]

---

[8] This is observed by Keith Campbell, 'Colours', p. 147. The bearing of this
consequence of a subjectivist conception of colour upon statements of colour
incompatibility will be taken up in chapter 3.

It may be objected that the relativity just indicated is incompatible with the fact that we acknowledge a distinction between the real and apparent colour (or taste) of a thing. We do indeed make such a distinction, but it is important to see that it is drawn quite differently from the distinction between real and apparent shape or size. In the latter case, there is an experience-independent criterion for whether the primary quality is instantiated, viz. measurement; but for secondary qualities the distinction is drawn from *within* the realm of appearance, by reference to experiences taken as standard. To suffer an illusion with respect to colour is for your colour experience not to match that of a normal perceiver in normal conditions; and we can easily imagine circumstances in which the standard of normality might shift, so that what was once counted as illusory now counts as veridical. And of course this is what the dispositional thesis leads us to expect. Consider what we should say of a simplified practice of colour ascription in which there is just one perceiver with constant illumination and visual receptivity: in such a case it seems that there is no way for a distinction between real and apparent colour to arise, since there is no departure from the standard set by this solitary perceiver's experience. But we can certainly suppose our solitary perceiver to suffer illusions as to the primary qualities of things. We shall not, then, significantly misrepresent the nature of secondary qualities if we stick with the simple equation of having the quality and seeming to have it; just as we do not misrepresent the nature of poisonousness by saying simply that poisonous things are disposed to cause ill-health in animals—even though there are special and essentially untypical circumstances in which they do not. It is a conceptual truth that red things *typically* look red.[9]

[9] I do not wish to suggest that our drawing a distinction between the real and apparent secondary qualities of a thing is of no philosophical interest, nor that the principles on which this distinction is drawn are simple and easily stated. It is just that at the level of generality at which I shall be operating the distinction and its basis can be safely neglected; the fundamental observer-dependence of secondary qualities will be preserved in any more refined account of the real–apparent distinction.

If the dispositional thesis is correct, we can also predict that a certain kind of scepticism about secondary qualities is incoherent. It makes sense to suggest that we might be systematically in error about the primary qualities of things —a Cartesian demon may interfere with our sense organs in such a way as to make things seem otherwise than they are. But this is not possible for secondary qualities, since their presence is constituted by how things sensorily seem— the Cartesian demon cannot contrive to make us wrong about the colours and tastes of things. The difference here is that no amount of information gleaned from within experience can logically entail which are the primary qualities of an object, but we *can* deduce from the character of our experience which secondary qualities a thing has. We might say that scepticism is ruled out for secondary qualities because (roughly) phenomenalism is correct for them; but phenomenalism is not similarly correct for primary qualities, and so scepticism can get a foothold.[10] The only kind of scepticism appropriate to secondary qualities would be, in effect, a scepticism about other minds: for if the experiences of others in a perceptual group to which one belongs set the standard for correct ascriptions of colour, then one can only know if one's own experiences are veridical by knowing how other people experience things. However, as we just observed, the community-based criterion of correctness is itself a superficial feature of secondary quality ascriptions, and so no deep-going scepticism afflicts such ascriptions.

A close corollary of the last point is that secondary qualities do not have the distinctive characteristics of natural kinds: in particular, they are not reducible to possibly unknown 'internal structures' or 'real essences'.[11] Colours, for

---

[10] We can say something stronger: phenomenalism about secondary qualities can be correct only because it is *not* correct for primary qualities. For the disposition in which being red consists needs an explanatory basis of primary qualities (wavelengths etc.), and these cannot in turn be construed as dispositions to produce certain experiences—on pain of there being no non-circular explanation of the occurrence of *those* experiences.

[11] The contrary view is held by David Armstrong, *A Materialist Theory of the Mind*, chap. 12; and Saul Kripke, *Naming and Necessity*, p. 140, note 71.

example, are not to be identified with wavelengths of the spectrum. This is simply because the dispositional thesis defines colours in terms of sensory appearances, and so we cannot envisage cases in which the identity of a given colour comes apart from its appearance—there cannot be 'fool's red' as there can be fool's gold. In this respect secondary qualities are like sensations.[12] This point can be driven home by giving a variable realisation argument against reductive identification. Suppose we discovered that the physical properties of the surfaces of red-looking objects varied in some fairly radical way but that the variation was compensated for in our visual receptors: we would not then say that the objects varied in colour, contrary to what we had supposed on the basis of their appearance; we would say rather that the property of being red was correlated with no single underlying physical property. That is, we would say that objects look red, and so are red, in virtue of *different* 'categorical bases' in those objects—the disposition to produce a given kind of experience has a variable ground. The independence of secondary qualities from their physical ground in the object can be obscured by failing to distinguish two ways in which a quality can be associated with a disposition to produce experiences, which we can call intrinsic and extrinsic. It is true that if an object has a primary quality it will be

Thomas Reid seems to hold a very similar view: see *Essays on the Intellectual Powers of Man*, II, XVII.

[12] Armstrong proposes to treat secondary qualities and sensations in the same way: he suggests a 'contingent (*sic*) identity' between colours and underlying physical properties, thus allowing (as he thinks) for the possibility that the 'redness of [a] surface should vary independently of the physical properties of the surface', ibid., p. 274. Kripke evidently wishes to treat the cases of 'yellow' and 'pain' differently, holding that 'looks yellow' serves merely to fix the reference of 'yellow' while 'feels like pain' enters into the meaning of 'pain': the former pair can therefore come apart, the latter cannot. Kripke thus commits himself to the claim that in a possible world in which what are actually yellow things look systematically red it is right to call those things 'yellow' in *that* world. It is hard to avoid the conclusion that Kripke has overgeneralised his doctrine of natural kinds here. Certainly there is no *necessity* that *all* general terms should conform to the reference-fixing model: we can, if we like, simply *stipulate* a language in which property terms are introduced in the dispositional way—my position is then that *our* colour terms are just as they would be under such a stipulation.

disposed to produce experiences as of that quality under certain conditions; but this disposition is extrinsic to the quality, in the sense that the type of experience is not constitutive of the object's having the quality—it is merely one causal consequence of it. In the case of secondary qualities, the disposition is intrinsic, in the sense that there is no independent characterisation of what it is to have the quality from which the disposition to produce experiences flows. If we confuse these two ways a quality can be dispositional in respect of experience, we will be inclined to think that the secondary quality disposition must have a categorical basis in the object in just the way the primary quality disposition does—that is, we will suppose there to be a reduction of the disposition to its causal ground in the object. But in the case of secondary qualities, the most we should demand is that for any instantiation of such a quality there should be *some* ground in the object which explains (in conjunction with certain other facts) the perceiver's experience; we should not expect the stronger proposition that there is one such ground for any instantiation of the quality. I suspect that confusion on this point is what makes some people wish to combine a Lockean dispositional thesis about colour with a reduction of colour to physical properties of surfaces; but in fact such a reduction is ruled out once the Lockean thesis is properly understood—colours are *intrinsically* dispositional.[13]

It is often observed that secondary qualities are explanatorily idle, and in two ways. First, these qualities are not ascribed to things as part of the enterprise of explaining the causal interactions of objects with each other: colour and taste do not contribute to the causal powers of things.

[13] This mistake seems to be made by Michael Dummett, 'Common Sense and Physics', pp. 34–5, and by Gareth Evans, 'Things Without the Mind', p. 95. Kripke (loc. cit.) is well aware of the tension, writing 'it is especially important to realize that yellowness is not a dispositional property, although it is related to a disposition'. Consider the analogy with pain-patches (see note 5 above): it would obviously be wrong to acknowledge the inherent dispositionality of 'paininess' and at the same time insist upon a theoretical identification of that property with some supposed underlying basis.

Primary qualities are precisely the qualities that figure in such explanations; that is why the physical sciences speak of primary qualities, but not secondary qualities, in formulating the laws governing objects. Secondly, secondary qualities do not explain our perception of them; primary qualities are what do that. Both of these features of secondary qualities can be seen to follow directly from the dispositional thesis. The first feature issues from the fact that the interactions between objects proceed independently of the experiences of perceivers, and these are definitive of secondary qualities. Objects would behave in the same way if there were no perceivers to constitute their secondary qualities; and varying appearance to different perceivers does not affect the object's causal powers in relation to other objects. The second feature issues from the nature of causal explanation: since being red is analysed as looking red, we cannot explain why something looks red by saying that it is red, for this involves an explanatory circle; it is like explaining why a substance poisoned someone by saying it is poisonous. Such 'explanations' may not be entirely vacuous, because they suggest that the cited dispositional property operates similarly in other cases; but we know that something more substantial must be available, if only because we also want to explain why things have these effects in general. Primary qualities are then called in to do the explaining secondary qualities cannot manage themselves. This is why it is strictly wrong to say that a red object is disposed to produce experiences as of its looking red in virtue of its being *red*; the analogous claim about primary qualities, on the other hand, is perfectly correct.[14]

With these (largely familiar) features of secondary qualities noted, let us now turn to indexicals; we shall see that they share certain features of secondary qualities (or analogues of them).

Indexicality is often cited as the paradigm of that which a properly objective conception of the world would exclude: the physicist, we are told, refrains from indexical description

[14] Cf. Bennett, op. cit., pp. 102 f.

of the world.[15] The intuitive reason for this exclusion is that the use of indexicals involves treating oneself as somehow a *centre*, as a privileged coordinate; an objective description should not be thus invidious in its depiction of reality—it must be impartial. Indexicals flout this requirement of objective centreless description because they are semantically relative in their interpretation. It is clear, then, that indexicals are not to figure in what Bernard Williams calls the '*absolute* conception' of the world.[16] Similarly, secondary qualities cannot figure in the absolute conception on account of their relativity to the perceiver. But it does not yet follow that indexicals are subjective. We have a pair of distinctions at play here—absolute/relative, objective/subjective—and it is a substantive question whether they coincide at any point. The subjectivity of secondary qualities implies their relativity, since the same objects could appear different to different perceivers and their subjective appearance fixes their identity. But it is, to say the least, not obvious that the relativity of indexicals implies their subjectivity, where the notion of subjectivity requires more than a dependence of semantic evaluation upon the speaker's context of utterance. If we are to make out a case for a more significant kind of subjectivity on the part of indexicals, then we shall need to explicate the idea of 'centredness' in some way which manifestly introduces a genuinely subjective element: the centre must not be just an objectively capturable location in the world but something distinctively subjective in nature. It will perhaps come as no surprise that I am going to suggest that the notion of the *self*—that which has a certain subjective

---

[15] Thus Russell tells us 'that no egocentric particulars occur in the language of physics. Physics views space–time impartially, as God might be supposed to view it; there is not, as in perception, a region which is specially warm and intimate and bright, surrounded in all directions by gradually growing darkness. A physicist will not say "I saw a table", but like Neurath or Julius Caesar, "Otto saw a table"; he will not say "A meteor is visible now", but "A meteor was visible at 8h. 43m. G.M.T.", and in this statement "was" is intended to be without tense.' *An Inquiry into Meaning and Truth*, chap. 7, p. 102.

[16] See his *Descartes, passim*, and 'Another Time, Another Place, Another Person'.

perspective on the world—constitutes the relevant conception of a centre.

I should first make it explicit that my primary interest is not in the semantics of indexical *expressions*; I am concerned with indexical thoughts, or better with the indexical modes of presentation which enter thoughts. That is, I am concerned with what it is to think of things as *I, here, now*, etc. Focusing on indexical modes of presentation helps to isolate the feature of indexicality I want to stress. If we concentrate upon indexical expressions we will be apt chiefly to notice that they are *occasional*, in the sense that their reference varies from occasion to occasion; but when we turn to indexical thought it is the *perspectival* character of indexical modes of presentation that stands out—the way they incorporate and reflect a 'point of view' on the world. This perspective is something possessed by a psychological subject; and it is the subjectivity of the subject that makes it proper to regard the indexical modes of presentation constitutive of a perspective as themselves subjective. The point may be put in this way: all the indexicals are linked with *I*, and the *I* mode of presentation is subjective in character because it comprises the special perspective a person has on himself. Very roughly, we can say that to think of something indexically is to think of it in relation to *me*, as I am presented to myself in self-consciousness: all indexical modes of presentation go back to, and are anchored in, conscious presentation of the subject of the indexical thought in question.[17] This intuitive picture of indexicals can be articulated and made more precise in various ways, which I shall now briefly allude to.

[17] This claim, and the refinements of it that follow, is stronger than is strictly needed for my purposes. I have chosen to express the egocentricity of indexicals by relating them to the *having* of I-thoughts, thus assuming that such thoughts are necessary for the possession of other indexical thoughts. Those who find this implausible (as I do not) could make do with a weaker claim, viz. that *our* understanding as theorists of a creature's indexical thoughts always involves relating the content of such thoughts to the thinking subject—as (it might be claimed) the thinker himself does not (or perhaps cannot). Alternatively, one might suggest that a counterfactual condition forges the required link: *were* the indexical thinker to have I-thoughts, *then* such-and-such relations would hold between these thoughts and his other indexical thoughts.

The strongest statement of the intuitive picture would be the thesis that we can and should *define* all the indexicals in terms of 'I'. Russell once made an instructive proposal to that effect: he suggested that we could define all indexicals in terms of 'I-now' (along with certain non-indexical expressions).[18] Russell's idea was to treat 'I-now' as an unstructured expression denoting something like momentary stages of the subject. In a suitably weak sense of 'define' I think Russell's suggestion is quite plausible, but I am not particularly concerned to urge the correctness of this approach. What I want to note is that such a system of definition would exhibit indexicals as tied to the first-person perspective in a very strong way; indeed 'I-now' has some claim to being more subjective in content than 'I', since momentary stages of the self have more of the characteristics of subjectivity than the continuant person. I also think that *if* we are out to define indexicals on a minimal basis then 'I-now' is a good choice of primitive, because it answers to the intuitive picture of the matter. However, we should jib at Russell's suggestion that 'I-now' be construed as a *semantic* primitive; he should have said that the definition requires *both* 'I' and 'now' as independent primitives. Here we may be reminded of the issue about the semantic compositeness of 'looks red'. It is tempting, though misguided, to try to fuse 'looks' and 'red' together in an effort to pick out something purely subjective, to avoid permitting the analysis of 'red' to make any apparent reference to what is outside the mind; it is similarly tempting to fuse 'I' and 'now' into a unitary expression whose interpretation does not go beyond the purely psychological.[19] If we can appreciate these temptations

---

[18] Actually, Russell opts for 'this' as his primitive indexical in chap. 7 of *An Inquiry into Meaning and Truth*; but he regards this chiefly as just a matter of convenience—'I-now' would do equally well, he says. We could then define 'this' as 'the object to which I now attend', 'here' as 'the place where I am now', 'I' as 'the self made up of a sequence of I-now stages', 'now' as 'the time contemporaneous with I-now', etc.

[19] We might diagnose these temptations as arising from the following quasi-ontogenetic speculations. In the case of perceptual experience there is a stage at which representational content is not differentiated from its mode of sensory

without succumbing to them, we thereby acknowledge the force of the subjectivist view of the two cases. The Russellian proposal thus seems to me to be an instructive exaggeration.

A weaker thesis may be extracted from a recent suggestion made by R. Chisholm and David Lewis (anticipated by S. Shoemaker).[20] They hold that all beliefs are self-ascriptive or self-locating: whenever you have a belief about an object you think of that object as standing in a relation to yourself. It does not seem to me that this relativity to self is built into the very semantics of *all* expressions with which one may express a belief, nor into the content of all types of mode of presentation of the objects of belief; but I do think the thesis has some plausibility for indexical beliefs, since a definite relation to the self *is* built into their content. This is weaker than the Russellian suggestion because the thesis that all indexical thought is implicitly *de se* (in Lewis's sense) does not immediately imply that we can define all indexicals in terms of 'I'. Again, I shall not unreservedly endorse this thesis as stated; I merely note that its *prima facie* attractiveness confirms the intuitive picture of the subject-centred character of indexical thought.[21]

representation: raw phenomenal properties are only subsequently structured according to mode and content. The differentiation might be said to occur when the perceiver's *judgements* about the external world begin to be sensitive in certain ways to aspects of his experience. Somewhat similarly, there is a stage at which the subject does not differentiate himself from his current time-slice; the present time is thus an integral part of the subject's conception of 'I'. The differentiation of self and time occurs when the subject comes to think of himself as a continuant object. In both cases the speculative thought is that there is a primitive conceptual level for the expression of which 'looks-red' and 'I-now' are not inappropriate; it is a level at which the distinction of mind and world has not yet been properly made. I do not know whether such speculations are psychologically correct, but I think something of the sort lies behind the urge to hyphenate which some philosophers give in to. However, even if these speculations were correct, they would not justify taking the phrases in question to be *semantic* primitives. (But a tendency to say similarly wrong things in two areas can be as indicative of analogy as the saying of similarly right things.)

[20] R. Chisholm, *The First Person*; David Lewis, 'Attitudes *De Dicto* and *De Se*'; S. Shoemaker, 'Self-Reference and Self-Awareness', esp. p. 567.

[21] Even if the thesis that all indexical thought directly involves self-ascriptive thought is found psychologically implausible, it is worth noting that it seems in principle *possible* for a thinker to frame his indexical thoughts explicitly as self-ascriptions.

The third and weakest way of forging a connexion between 'I' and the other indexicals is simply to claim that there are *a priori* links between them. We might put this by saying that indexicals cannot be independently mastered; their meanings are interrelated in a sort of 'holistic system' generating certain *a priori* truths. Thus one who has mastered the indexicals must appreciate the *a priori* status of 'I am here now', and this requires that 'here' and 'now' be understood as having the requisite semantic relation to 'I'.[22] This can be compared with the *a priori* status of '*x* is red iff *x* looks red': this is true *a priori* (and is indeed analytic) because 'red' is constitutively linked with 'looking red', and so the subjective nature of the latter expression accrues to the former. Similarly, the *a priori* analytic status of 'I am here now' depends upon relations of meaning between 'I' and the other indexicals, and so its subjective content indirectly attaches to them. This can be seen in the fact that replacing 'here' and 'now' by non-indexical specifications of the time and place referred to in a token utterance of 'I am here now' does not preserve the *a priori* analytic status of the sentence.

I hope that these brief remarks about the egocentricity of indexical modes of presentation have established an initial presumption that indexicals are subjective in something like the sense in which secondary qualities are. The analogy might be put as follows: to grasp what it is for an object to have a secondary quality or an indexical property one needs to appreciate what it is like to perceive secondary qualities or entertain egocentric modes of presentation—that is, appreciate this 'from the inside'. And this is because of the way sensory experience and the first-person perspective enter into the character of the respective ways in which the world

---

[22] Again, we can distinguish a stronger and a weaker thesis here: the stronger thesis says that mastery of indexicals other than 'I' presupposes mastery of 'I' and its semantic relations to those other indexicals; the weaker thesis says that *if* 'I' is mastered then the semantic relations to other indexicals must be recognised. I believe the stronger thesis, but the weaker thesis will suffice for the present point: the important consideration is just that 'I' *is* so related to 'here' and 'now', whoever appreciates the fact.

may be represented as being: the world is represented as having attributes whose existence and identity have their source in subjective aspects of the representer.[23] Not unnaturally, therefore, an objective description of the world will eschew these subject-involving representations. Later we shall observe certain features of the two cases which confirm this analogy in respect of subjectivity; for now let us note some parallels arising out of what has been said so far.

First, the relativity of secondary qualities and indexicals has the consequence that a difference of representation does not imply a genuine disagreement. There is, I said, no disagreement between Martians and us when they call green what we call red, and hence no error on either part; error would occur, indeed, only if a Martian with defective sight— by Martian standards—were to represent things visually just as we do, calling what is green for Martians red. Somewhat similarly, but much more obviously, two people in different places do not disagree if one calls 'here' what the other describes as 'there'; there would be disagreement only if they *both* referred to the same place as 'here'. In the loose sense favoured by Putnam, we could even say that secondary quality ascriptions are indexical—they are implicitly relative to *us now*; but this sense is too loose to warrant claiming any genuine *semantic* indexicality in secondary quality words (as indeed it is too loose to warrant Putnam's analogous claim about natural kind words).[24] In consequence of this

[23] This has the consequence that a purely objective being, such as we might suppose God to be, could not grasp what it is for an object to be red or a place to be here: for these properties can be grasped only by a being who has perceptual experiences of red things or who has a perspective on the world from within space and time—or if these can be grasped by a being lacking such advantages it is only by his (somehow) imaginatively putting himself into the position of one who is so advantaged.

Another (slightly incautious) way to state the subjectivity claim is simply to say that before there were conscious beings there were no secondary qualities and indexical properties; for these exist only in virtue of relations to subjects of consciousness.

[24] See Hilary Putnam, 'The Meaning of "Meaning"', pp. 229 f. Putnam's idea is that we fix the reference of a term like 'water' by stipulating that it is to refer to the substance instances of which are to be found *around here*. I might say, analogously, that 'red' is to have in its extension objects which are

relativity the request to complete an inventory of indexical properties or secondary qualities of some object must be understood as selecting a certain point of view as standard. Secondly, indexicals are like secondary qualities in not figuring in causal explanations of the interactions of physical objects: physics omits them not (or not just) because they are relative and egocentric; it omits them because they do not constitute explanatory predicates of a theory of the causal workings of nature. And again, this explanatory idleness appears to stem from the subject-involving character of indexical properties: indexical predicates do not attribute intrinsic physical properties to things, and so do not contribute to an account of the causal powers of things. Lastly, it seems absurd to suppose that indexicals might denote natural kinds and hence be reducible to real essences of things—as if we could discover that the things we had been calling 'here' were in fact of totally different natural kinds, so that we would have to declare the word ambiguous or speak of 'fool's here'! Indexical words just do not purport to function in this way; they serve rather to express a subjective perspective on the world. Secondary quality words likewise do not purport to identify appearance-transcendent natural kinds; they serve to record the ways the world subjectively strikes us. It is, then, the subject-involving character of indexicals which lies behind these three features, and this seems paralleled by the experience-involving nature of secondary qualities and the consequences of this.

Now that I have laid out the general conception of secondary qualities and indexical properties with which I shall be working, I can proceed to consider some issues relating to the two topics in the light of this conception. These should indirectly serve to explain and justify the conception further.

phenomenally similar to those that look red *to us now*; other speakers could determine a different extension for 'red' by making the same kind of reference-fixing stipulation—if, for example, green things (for us) looked red to Twin-earthians. Reasons for not declaring natural kind terms to be *themselves* semantically indexical are given by Tyler Burge, 'Other Bodies'; the same sorts of reasons apply to secondary quality terms.

3
The Laws of Subjectivity

Given that secondary qualities are subjective, any laws or principles governing them will have the status of laws of subjectivity: they will formulate how the world must be represented in experience. In this chapter I shall suggest a number of such laws and comment upon their significance; and I shall suggest something similar about indexicals.

Philosophers have often discussed the status of such propositions as 'no surface can be simultaneously red and green' and 'no substance can be simultaneously sweet and bitter'—propositions in which the possible co-instantiation of a pair of qualities is denied. It is generally agreed that such propositions are necessary and *a priori*; the point of contention has been whether they are analytic or synthetic. What is notable about these discussions is that the contrary qualities considered tend always to be secondary qualities; it is not usual to consider propositions like 'nothing can be simultaneously round and square'. Perhaps it is thought that incompatibilities of primary qualities are too obviously analytic, in which case it would be a fact of some significance that qualities differing in their analysis should also differ in this further respect. However, the question of the semantic status of these modal propositions is not my present concern; my concern is to argue that the secondary quality incompatibilities are indeed different in status from the primary quality incompatibilities, and that there is something special about the former—but different and special in another (though possibly connected[1])

[1] I have observed that people are more prone to try to construct ingenious counterexamples to colour incompatibilities than to shape incompatibilities (always in vain of course). Perhaps this is some evidence that the former are synthetic while the latter are analytic; for synthetic necessities always attract more contestation than analytic necessities. If there was this asymmetry, there would be the question *why* subjectively defined properties yield such synthetic necessities while objectively defined properties yield merely analytic necessities: but I shall not pursue the issue now.

way. My thesis is to be that (for example) colour incompatibilities are necessities of how the world can *seem* in perceptual experience, whereas shape incompatibilities are necessities of how the world can *be* independently of the possible content of experience. Just to have labels for these two kinds of necessity, let us say that the former are necessities of *phenomenology* while the latter are necessities of *ontology*. Before I give my reasons for applying this distinction to secondary qualities and primary qualities respectively, a word on the general distinction between necessities of seeming and necessities of being.

It is clear enough that the two sorts of modal proposition are quite distinct in purport: to ask how the world can be in itself is one kind of thing; to ask how it can seem to a perceiving consciousness is quite another. And on the face of it there seems no compelling reason why the answers we get to these questions should even be interdependent: perhaps there are ways the world can be which no form of awareness can perceptually represent, and ways the world cannot be which are capable of seeming to be the case. After all, the external world is a region of reality distinct from our consciousness of it, so why should they conform to the same modal laws? Moreover, we can produce examples in which the phenomenological and the ontological questions receive different and independent answers. Thus things can sometimes seem as they cannot be: the wooden lectern may seem to someone to be made of ice, but we know that it is necessarily not made of ice; Hesperus can seem distinct from Phosphorus, though they are necessarily identical; and an Escher drawing can make something look possible which reason persuades us could not occur in the world. Such cases are in a way unsurprising: experience can misrepresent how things are, so why should it not misrepresent how things *can* be? Experience is like reasoning in this respect: we can reason in violation of the necessary laws of logic, and this is to represent the world in thought as it cannot be in reality—we can certainly believe to be the case what is not in fact possible.

Conversely, might there not be ways the world can be and is which neither we nor any conceivable perceiving being could represent in experience? The natural model for this state of affairs would be certain perceptual illusions: it is (presumably) a psychological law of the human visual system that lines of equal length cannot seem to be so when they occur in the Muller–Lyer illusion. But there might also be cases which hold for any possible sensory system: consider the properties of elementary particles or of the whole universe; and some have supposed that physical space can be (indeed is) non-Euclidean in structure though visual sense must represent it in experience as Euclidean.[2] In general, there seems no *a priori* reason why every possible condition of the universe should be susceptible of sensory representation. So we should not expect any necessary coincidence between the modal laws of ontology and phenomenology.

To return to secondary qualities, I wish to argue that colour incompatibilities (etc.) state necessary truths about visual consciousness, whereas shape incompatibilities (etc.) state necessary truths about the experience-independent objective world. There are a number of ways of arguing for this contrast. It is noteworthy, to begin with, that writers on this subject are prone to gloss colour incompatibilities by appealing to the possible composition of a visual field, though they typically show no awareness of the significance of this way of conceiving the cases; and indeed I think that it is eminently natural to proceed in this way, as it is not for shape incompatibilities—this is a difference of treatment one naturally falls into.[3] My diagnosis of this tendency is that the subjectivity of secondary qualities is being implicitly acknowledged: we find ourselves asking whether a single surface could produce *experiences* as of contrary colours. Implicit recognition of the relativity of secondary qualities, in contrast to primary qualities, also directs one to consider the properties of sensory field in the former case but not in the latter:

---

[2] Such a view is suggested by P. F. Strawson, *The Bounds of Sense*, pp. 281 ff.
[3] See, e.g. Moritz Schlick, 'Form and Content', p. 353.

for, as I observed in chapter 2, there is a sense in which the same surface can be both red and green, the same substance both sweet and bitter, since the objects in question may present these contrary appearances to different perceivers. Compare the proposition 'nothing can be both poisonous and nourishing': unless we hear this as implicitly relative to some particular choice of creature, it sounds (and is) just false. In (rightly) dismissing this kind of objection to claims about colour and taste incompatibility, we will need to relativise the colour and taste predicates to a perceiver, the same perceiver for both qualities; and this will have us considering how things can sensorily seem. Thus the underlying form of 'no surface can be red and green' is 'no surface can be red for a perceiver x at time t and also be green for x at t'; no such relativisation is required for 'nothing can be round and square'. It might be said that such relativisation to a perceiver does not yet introduce explicitly phenomenological considerations into the stated impossibility; but in fact we need a further relativisation which does explicitly involve us in phenomenology. For consider such familiar cases as that of experiencing the same water as hot with one hand and cold with another, or something producing different tastes as it stimulates different taste receptors: here we seem to have a single subject for whom the same thing has contrary secondary qualities. If we are to protect the assertion of incompatibility from such counterexamples, we shall need to have recourse to something like the idea of a point or region in a sensory field: the proper formulation will then be that at no point of a sensory field can red and green be (i.e. appear to be) instantiated, and similarly for the other cases. Once the relativisation to a sensory point or region is introduced, the phenomenological character of the claimed incompatibility of secondary qualities becomes inescapable; none of this is required for the likes of shape incompatibility.[4] But the most

---

[4] Note that the requisite notion of sensory region cannot be explained in physical terms. For suppose a given physical surface produces a kind of double vision in which the perceiver has an experience as of a red surface and an experience as of a green surface. Then it does not seem wrong to allow that the surface

direct argument for the phenomenological status of colour incompatibility is provided simply by taking the dispositional thesis seriously: since we can anlyse 'red' in terms of 'looks red', we can substitute the analysans into our modal proposition, thus obtaining 'no surface can look red to a given perceiver and simultaneously look green'. In other words, the dispositional analysis of colour interprets colour incompatibility as an incompatibility of seeming; no such interpretation is licensed by the correct analysis of primary qualities—quite the opposite. So we can say that what it *is* for colours and tastes to exclude other colours and tastes is for it to be impossible that things should *appear* to instantiate such combinations of qualities; whereas what it is for shapes and sizes to exclude other shapes and sizes is for it to be impossible that things *have*, independently of appearance, such combinations of qualities.

This asymmetry can be made vivid by considering what would be the consequences of denying the two kinds of impossibility. Suppose, *per impossibile*, that things could be simultaneously round and square: what further impossibilities would then ensue? Well, in the latter case theoretical and common-sense mechanics would break down: there would be no coherent description of how bodies are disposed to interact—what, for example, would be the result of trying to put a square peg into a round hole? That such combinations should be ruled out is constitutive of there being an intelligible objective world of causally interacting objects. But the case is otherwise for secondary qualities: since they are irrelevant to the causal powers of things, the joint instantiation of contrary such qualities would not have these calamitous consequences for mechanics; things would, it seems, interact with each other just as before. What would be

is seen; but this case is not properly construed as a counterexample to the claim that no surface (or part thereof) can be red and green for a perceiver at a given time. What we should say is that in such a case the perceiver does not have an experience *as of* a surface in a single part of which red and green are instantiated together: that is, the correct formulation should be that no *phenomenal* surface can be red and green for a perceiver at a given time.

impossible in the circumstances supposed would be any *perception* of objects: we cannot imagine what it would be like to experience things as having contrary secondary qualities. This difference of repercussions indicates that we are dealing with distinct kinds of necessity.[5]

I must immediately add, however, that there is not, for these laws of phenomenology and ontology, the kind of independence I said was possible in principle for the two kinds of necessity and which I illustrated by example. For we do also want to say that nothing can *be* both red and green, and that nothing can *seem* both round and square. By now this interdependence ought to strike us as somewhat remarkable— that is, if my claims about the status of the different cases and the general independence of seeming and being have been accepted. It must seem a non-trivial fact that the necessities of ontology and phenomenology coincide at this point. But I do not think the coincidence refutes the claimed difference of interpretation; what we need is a distinction between the grounds and the consequences of the respective impossibilities. The ground of the impossibility of being in the case of secondary qualities is the conceptually prior impossibility of seeming; the ground of the impossibility of seeming in the primary quality case is the conceptually prior impossibility of being: that is, ground and consequence are reversed in the two cases. This distinction is motivated by the analyses of primary and secondary qualities I adopted earlier. In the latter case, the impossibility of being flows from the dispositional analysis plus the impossibility of seeming; in the former case, the impossibility of seeming flows from the impossibility of being plus some non-trivial property of experience as a vehicle for the representation of the objective qualities of things.[6]

[5] One might have thought that these phenomenological necessities would be of special interest to the phenomenologists. But in fact their basic methodology precludes making the sort of distinction I have insisted upon: for all necessities are interpreted phenomenologically by them, including such cases as shape incompatibility. One looks in vain in Husserl's writings for any recognition of the *distinctively* phenomenological status of secondary quality incompatibilities.

[6] The impossibility that something should seem round and square is, of

The interpretation I have offered of secondary quality incompatibility bears upon the question of the correct description of cases in which it is tempting to speak of a divided mind, as when a person's brain has been split into two functioning units.[7] Suppose such a person has his left eye stimulated with a given surface in such a way that the surface will look red to him, and suppose his right eye is stimulated by the same surface so as to make it look green. Then someone who wishes to hold that we have to do in such cases with a single conscious subject possessed of a unitary visual field is committed to the consequence that the surface looks red and green to the same subject in the same sensory region at the same time. But if that were so, then the proposition that nothing could be red and green would not, on my analysis of the purport of that proposition, be necessary after all. But we know antecedently that it *is* necessary; so the supposition of a unitary visual subject must be rejected. In other words, my interpretation of colour incompatibility shows that it is wrong to think that in split brain cases we have a single (visual) subject: if something looks red to x and looks green to y, then we know that x and y are not identical.[8] In the case of shape incompatibility we do not

course, to be understood as relative to a single sense modality: it is not to be denied that an object could look square and feel round simultaneously. (It is not necessary to add this qualification in the case of secondary quality incompatibility because these qualities are sense-specific.) It seems to me to be a substantive question why there cannot *seem* to be primary quality incompatibility. In this connexion note that this necessary feature of experience is hard to accommodate in the context of a belief acquisition theory of perceptual content, since it seems quite possible to *believe* of some object that it is square while simultaneously believing it is round—and this shows that it is some special property of perceptual experience, and not just of intentional states in general, that generates these impossibilities of seeming.

[7] For a discussion of these cases see Nagel, 'Brain Bisection and the Unity of Consciousness'.

[8] This reason for favouring the 'two minds' description of these cases is different from the reasons usually offered. The phenomena usually supposed to conflict with the single mind description have to do with a lack of integration and co-operation between the two hemispheres in the execution of various tasks—there is extreme dissociation of the components of normally integrated skills. My point, however, is stronger: it is that the single mind description involves denying a logical necessity.

have this constitutive connexion with the individuation of conscious subjects; it is more proper to say in this case that if an object x is square and an object y is round then x and y cannot be the same object. This is not to say we do not have *consequences* for the individuation of subjects and objects flowing from incompatibilities not directly defined with respect to those entities; the point is rather that it is internal to the two sorts of impossibility—of ontology and phenomenology—that they should be thus related to the identity of objects and subjects, respectively.

Those philosophers holding a reductionist view of secondary qualities will disagree with my phenomenological interpretation of colour incompatibility. D. Armstrong indeed claims it as a virtue of his reductionist account that it can explain secondary quality incompatibility as simply a special case of primary quality incompatibility: thus he suggests that being red might be identifiable with having a fine grid, while being green is identifiable with having a coarse grid, and these grids are incompatible.[9] I have already rejected such a reductionist account and with it this type of explanation of colour incompatibility. But there is a weaker version of Armstrong's suggestion which is not immediately at variance with the position I have adopted on the nature of secondary qualities, and it is worth seeing why even this weaker version fails to give an adequate account of colour incompatibility. The idea is to find an objective correlate for each instance in which secondary qualities exclude each other: this objective correlate can vary from case to case and so is not claimed to be identical with the secondary quality concerned. Thus the primary quality ground of the disposition in which an instance of being red consists might be said to be incompatible with the (or any) corresponding ground for being green, these cases being possibly different from one instantiation of the colour to the next. This idea might be supplemented by

[9] Armstrong, *A Materialist Theory of the Mind*, pp. 279–80. Campbell suggests something similar in 'Colours', p. 139, though not in support of an objectivist account of colour.

including the physical character of a perceiver's sense organs in the objective correlate, so that looking red and looking green will always have *some* incompatible realisation in the perceiver's physiology.[10] If this type of suggestion were plausible, it would undermine my thesis that the necessities in question are *sui generis*, deriving from the nature of subjective perceptual consciousness. But is it plausible?

I find three faults in the idea. First, by weakening the claim to avoid reductionism we sacrifice an intuitive unity in what is asserted by 'nothing can be red and green simultaneously': we have to suppose that this proposition is true in virtue of a disjunctive proposition, itself open-ended, listing all the actual and possible primary quality grounds and their incompatibilities. But it seems evident that the original sentence expresses a single impossibility concerning the co-instantiation of just two qualities. If we try to repair this fault by construing the colour predicates as carrying an existential quantification over objective correlates, to the effect that for each instantiation of the colour in question there is some corresponding primary quality which excludes the instantiation of the primary quality corresponding to the other colour, then we lose the specificity of the original necessity—it will not on this construal be making a modal claim about a particular identified quality. So we do not get a proper view of the content of the modal claim on this suggestion. Second, it is unclear that we can preserve the epistemic status of the necessity under this analysis of its purport. The original proposition is an *a priori* truth, assent to which does not require empirical knowledge of the grounds of the secondary qualities in question. But the suggestion under consideration requires us to know two empirical facts: which primary quality ground correlates with the given secondary qualities, and that these grounds are

---

[10] We shall need this supplementation anyway to deal with the point that the *same* physical (kind of) surface could look red on some occasions and look green on others, on account of differences of visual reactions.

indeed incompatible. The former is obviously an empirical question, and it seems that we could only appreciate the necessity, so construed, if we knew which primary qualities the necessity properly concerns; it would be too much like mere speculation otherwise. The latter point depends upon what sorts of primary quality ground are turned up; but it does not seem settleable ahead of time that the grounds of red and green should be *a priori* incompatible—perhaps it will be an empirical question whether the physical bases in the object are exclusive of one another. In short, our reasons for being convinced of the original proposition seem independent of the empirical issues raised by the explanation in terms of objective correlates: we would accept the *a priori* incompatibility of red and green no matter how things turned out empirically.[11] Third, there is some doubt even about whether there are corresponding necessities at the level of primary quality grounds: are we sure that it will turn out that the grounds of red and green are incompatible? Suppose, to change the example, we discovered that things taste sweet to us because of molecules with smooth bumps on them, and that things taste bitter because the molecules have sharp spikes: it might be that no molecules with both smooth bumps and sharp spikes exist, even as a matter of natural law, but that it is logically possible that they should. But if they were to exist we would have to say, on the present suggestion, that something *could* be sweet and bitter simultaneously— which contradicts what we had supposed necessary. But I do not think we could thus discover that such secondary qualities are compatible, contrary to what we initially supposed. The lesson of all this is that we are looking in the wrong place for the source of the necessity we recognised in the original proposition.

---

[11] Since Armstrong holds that the real nature of the properties of red and green is not given in perception but is a matter for scientific enquiry, he *has* to say that the question of colour incompatibility is an empirical question: it is a mere empirical speculation which might prove false—'nothing could be red and green' would have the same kind of epistemic status as 'nothing can be frozen and explosive'.

Neither are these faults removed by supplementing the alleged objective correlates with considerations about the perceiver's physiology. We again have the problem of unity, since distinct brain states could be correlated with an object's looking red.[12] The *a priori* character of the incompatibility is not preserved, for reasons analogous to those applicable to the primary quality ground in the object. And it does not seem guaranteed that looking red and looking green should be correlated with logically incompatible brain states: for might we not discover that it is conceptually or logically possible for a creature's brain to be in both of the states we find to correlate with these perceptual experiences? Again, we would not think it fit to reject the phenomenological necessity because we found the objective correlates in the brain not to exhibit a corresponding incompatibility; so we cannot claim to find a basis for the former in facts about the latter. Put differently, the laws of subjectivity seem not to be capturable in physicalistic terms.[13] I therefore think that the project of explaining secondary quality incompatibility as a special case of primary quality incompatibility cannot work, and so I conclude that the phenomenological status of the former is not threatened.

The view of colour incompatibility I have defended can

[12] This is just the familiar point that any mental state could have different physical realisations in different creatures' brains: see Putnam, 'The Nature of Mental States'.

[13] A different way of trying to explain the laws of subjectivity in physical terms would be by invoking functionalist theories of mental states. I do not believe, however, that this significantly improves upon the physicalist proposal I have already discussed: perhaps the unity objection is overcome by the functionalist reduction, but the epistemic and modal points remain. There is also the problem (to which I recur in chapter 8, section ii) that the same functional characterisation may be compatible with different colour experiences: the experiences would have incompatible contents, but their functional properties would not be incompatible—for they would be identical. However, it is difficult properly to evaluate the functionalist account of the laws of subjectivity without embarking upon a general evaluation of functionalism as a theory of mind: my suspicion is that in attempting to give a functionalist account of the laws of subjectivity the inadequacies of that theory will become yet more evident than they already are. For a critical discussion of functionalism see Ned Block, 'Troubles with Functionalism', and my 'Functionalism and Phenomenalism: a critical note'.

be compared with Wittgenstein's treatment of 'the logic of colour'.[14] Wittgenstein is concerned with the 'internal relations' between colours which establish what he calls a 'mathematics of colour'—in particular, relations of kinship and contrast between colours.[15] He also discusses various examples of impossible colours, e.g. reddish green and (most extensively) transparent white. (Surprisingly, he does not in *Remarks on Colour* discuss colour incompatibility, which one might have thought an important case of the type of necessity with which he is concerned.) Wittgenstein interprets these necessary *a priori* truths as 'laws of appearance' and constantly glosses them as truths about how things can look, even speaking of them as 'phenomenological' in character.[16] He does not, however, remark that colours are secondary qualities in the traditional Lockean sense, nor does he contrast the laws of appearance governing them with necessities involving primary qualities.[17] But it seems to me that the quasi-logical propositions about colour he considers should be awarded the kind of status I have ascribed to colour incompatibility: they are necessary truths governing the form of perceptual experience and are to be contrasted with necessary truths of a superficially similar character concerning primary qualities.[18] I would say, then, that each sense

[14] Wittgenstein, *Remarks on Colour*, and *Zettel* §§ 331–70. Cf. Schlick, 'Form and Content'.

[15] He says: ' "There is no such thing as a reddish green" is akin to the sentences that we use as axioms in mathematics.' *Zettel*, § 346. Also: 'We have a colour system as we have a number system. Do the systems reside in *our* nature or in the nature of things?' ibid., § 357.

[16] See esp. *Remarks on Colour*: e.g., 'But what kind of proposition is that, that blending in white removes the colouredness from the colour? As I mean it, it can't be a proposition of physics. There the temptation to believe in a phenomenology, something midway between science and logic, is very great.' II, 3.

[17] He does, however, show a marked tendency to approach the topic of colour qualities through colour experience, and indeed remarks 'The colour concepts are to be treated like the concepts of sensations', ibid. III, 72.

[18] I suppose that geometry, as a theory of physical space, comprises a body of such necessary truths about primary qualities. Propositions like 'there can't be a four-sided ellipse' or 'an ellipse is more like a circle than a triangle' might be examples of propositions superficially similar to the phenomenological necessities we have discussed. (It is notable how much less interesting, i.e. more trivial, such propositions are than those affirming secondary quality necessities.)

brings with it a system of secondary qualities exhibiting quasi-logical relations which arise from the subjective nature of the experience involved, these relations not being reducible to anything objective. If we were to describe the world as it is independently of experience, we would have no inkling of these laws of subjectivity; it is only when we enquire what it is like to have conscious experience of the world that these modal laws are disclosed. In other words, we can grasp the laws of subjectivity only by enjoying the kinds of experience of secondary qualities from which they issue.[19] By contrast, necessary truths about primary qualities are appreciable independently of taking up any particular perceptual view of the world—their source is non-sensory.

The Wittgensteinian 'laws of appearance' raise questions parallel to those I discussed in connexion with colour incompatibility. Consider the impossibility of a transparent white object: I would explicate this as the impossibility that a surface *look* to a given perceiver both white and transparent.[20] Now someone might challenge this interpretation by invoking split brain cases: we imagine a case in which a given surface is made to look white to one eye and also made to look transparent to the other eye—will it not look both transparent and white to the same perceiver? The obvious answer is that all this case shows is that we cannot associate a unitary perceptual subject with a divided brain: the proposition that a surface cannot look transparent and white in effect imposes a necessary condition on what it is to have a single visual field. The question of reducibility

---

[19] Suppose that bats have a language for their perceptual sensations, and suppose that we do not know what it is like to have the sensations about which we hear them discourse. Then, although we know that the bats have words for the corresponding secondary qualities which figure in specific laws of subjectivity, we cannot grasp what those laws are: only when we know what it is like for bats to perceive those secondary qualities will we be in a position to predict which sentences of theirs express *a priori* necessities concerning the denoted qualities. But we can understand the geometrical necessities they express without any inkling of the specific content of their experience.

[20] In citing this example of Wittgenstein's I do not mean to suggest that it is entirely uncontroversial, nor that it does not call for some kind of elucidation: it is intended illustratively.

also arises for Wittgenstein's examples: is it possible to explain the necessary character of these truths in non-phenomenological terms? Exactly analogous objections apply in these cases as applied in the case of secondary quality incompatibility: whether the unity and specificity of the original proposition can be captured; whether its epistemic status is preserved; whether we can guarantee the existence of a corresponding necessity at the physical level. An especially tempting objectivist reduction for the case of transparent white goes as follows: for a surface to be transparent is for it to let through the incident light, whereas for it to be white is for it to reflect all of the light; so transparent white is impossible because a surface cannot simultaneously interact in both these ways with the light incident upon it. But now consider the case of a Martian whose visual apparatus is so constructed that he has an experience as of something white when light from what *we* call the green part of the spectrum enters his eye. Given the relativity of ascriptions of colour, it seems we must allow that such surfaces are white for Martians, i.e. they speak truly when they ascribe whiteness to these (green for us) surfaces. But then, according to the physical explanation just suggested, the Martian ought to be able to envisage the possibility of a transparent white surface; it ought to be just as conceivable to him as a transparent green surface is to us. But of course this just contradicts the acknowledged necessity of the non-existence of transparent white surfaces. I think this shows that the impossibility of transparent white cannot be explained in this objective way: the content of the impossibility is just that nothing could *look* transparent and white—and the Martians would agree with us about *this* impossibility. As Wittgenstein says, though there are certain connexions between the laws of appearance and physical laws, the former cannot be explained or analysed in terms of the latter.[21] The proper

---

[21] He says: 'How must something look for it to appear to us coloured and transparent? This is not a question of physics, but it is connected with physical questions.' Also: 'Phenomenological analysis (as e.g. Goethe would have it) is

explanation is that in coming to be a conscious perceiver you come to conform to a rich system of phenomenological laws governing how things can seem, these laws arising from the very nature of perceptual experience. To say this is really only to spell out a consequence of the subjectivist view of secondary qualities, since the laws applicable to secondary qualities will be subjective in origin if those qualities are themselves subjectively constituted. All I have done here is to put together (as others have not) the idea of 'internal relations' between colours, tastes, etc., with the thesis that these are secondary qualities in the traditional sense.

I argued in chapter 2 that indexicals are subjective in the sense that they express the perspective of the speaker or thinker; I now want to make some remarks about the logic of indexicals in the light of this perspectival view of their significance. The idea of a logic of indexicals is the idea that indexical expressions may be treated as logical constants whose meaning determines certain sentences to be logical truths.[22] Comparably, the idea of modal logic (say) is to treat modal expressions as logical constants and study the logical truths determined by their meaning. In the case of modal logic we can say that modal logical truths reflect *a priori* truths about the nature of necessity and possibility (or about particular kinds of such)—modal logic is, if you like, a *theory* of necessity and possibility. But what is the proper interpretation of indexical logic: what intuitive notion or notions does it attempt to characterise? I want to suggest that indexical logic characterises what it is to have a first-person perspective, rather as modal logic characterises what is involved in (the notions of) necessity and possibility. Indexical logic is the logic (or theory) of modes of indexical presentation; it tells us how any subject must represent the world

analysis of concepts and can neither agree with nor contradict physics.' *Remarks on Colour*, III, 252 and II, 16, respectively. Wittgenstein does not, however, offer any argument such as I have offered for this thesis.

[22] David Kaplan seems to have been the originator of the idea of a logic of indexicals: see his well-known unpublished monograph, *Demonstratives*.

from a certain structured perspective.[23] Thus consider 'I am here now', 'I am not you', 'what happened in the past is not in the future', 'what is here is not also there', and so on. We can explicate these logical truths as expressing *a priori* necessities concerning modes of presentation: they record what particular types of mode of presentation involve and exclude, and so how the world can be represented from the point of view of a subject.[24] The claim that indexical logical truths express the constitutive interrelations of subjective modes of presentation stands in some contrast with another conception of what indexical logic is the logic (or theory) of—namely, the idea that it is the 'logic of *context*'. David Kaplan, for example, explains indexical validity as truth in any context of utterance: indexical sentences typically vary in truth-value from context to context—an indexical logical truth is one that cannot be uttered falsely.[25] This conception encourages the idea that indexical logic primarily studies the dependence of semantic interpretation on context, and so indexical validity consists in the circumstance that contextual interpretation always yields truth. It is certainly not incorrect to conceive of indexicality in this way, but I would make two points about the significance of this way of

[23] Tense logic based upon the indexical operators 'In the past', 'In the future', 'In the present' would fall under this general characterisation too.

[24] These claims of indexical incompatibility need to be formulated with some care: in the case of 'I am not you' the idea is that someone who refers to (or thinks of) x as 'I' and y as 'you' is (logically) committed to the distinctness of x and y; and similarly for 'what is here is not also there'. This commitment might conceivably turn out to be incorrect, as in a case in which, unknown to you, the person with whom you are speaking is really yourself on a tape recorder or the person you are looking at is really a reflection of you in a mirror: but the point is that in such cases the use of 'you' would have to be withdrawn. Contrast 'you' with 'that person' (or 'there' with 'that place'): it is perfectly legitimate knowingly to refer to oneself as 'that person' (though perhaps rather odd); but the sense of 'you' *requires* that it be applied only to another—which is not to say that mistakes are impossible. A symmetrical point holds for 'I': its sense requires application only to oneself, but it is possible to be mistaken about who one is (see chapter 4 for more on this).

[25] Actually, Kaplan's official view is that an indexical logical truth is a sentence (not utterance) which is true with respect to any context in which it is *set*; this modification is introduced in order to handle arguments composed of sequences of indexical sentences. But for present purposes we can ignore this refinement.

approaching the matter. First, the two notions of logical truth—truth with respect to any perspective and truth in any context—are arguably not equivalent in the indexical logical truths they select. The latter definition includes 'I am speaking' (or 'I am thinking' if the definition is applied at the level of thought) as indexically valid, since this sentence will be true whenever it is uttered and its interpretation depends upon context.[26] But this seems to me undesirable because the universal truth of this sentence depends not just on the meaning of 'I' but also upon that of 'speaking' (or 'thinking'), and this is not itself an indexical expression: so 'I am speaking' does not belong with the authentically (because purely) indexical logical truths cited just now. The perspectival conception excludes this undesirable case because it requires an indexical logical truth to turn solely upon the essential properties of indexical modes of presentation. The difference comes about because the intuitive interpretation of indexical logic is, in the one case, the notion of truth in any context of utterance and, in the other, the notion of what is determined by the interrelations of indexical modes of presentation. Secondly, even if the 'logic of context' interpretation did not differ in this extensional way from the 'logic of modes of presentation' interpretation, I think that a clear view of the nature of indexical logical truth requires us to register this feature of indexicality: being perspectival is as important to the meaning of indexicals as being semantically context-dependent.[27]

Conceiving indexical logic as expressing *a priori* necessary truths about how the world is indexically presented in thought allows us to make an analogy with what we said of secondary qualities: they both concern how the world can be

[26] Someone might suggest invoking the distinction between sentences true in any context and utterances of sentences that can never be false in any context in order to sidestep the 'I am speaking' case: but this seems *ad hoc* and still leaves 'I am thinking' (or 'I am a conscious being' if sleeping thinkers are counted as legitimate contexts).

[27] I do not wish to exaggerate my difference from Kaplan here; the point is really one of emphasis.

represented to someone. This is especially clear for incompatibilities of subjective view: the impossibility of being red and green is comparable with the impossibility of being here and there, in that both are to be explained by reference to how things can be presented to a subject—they are laws of subjectivity. An objective description of the world would afford no hint of the logic of modes of presentation because it would have no place for indexicals; just as an objective description would omit the logic of secondary qualities because it would not include them within its purview. And again, we arrive at this conception of laws of subjective modes of presentation by combining the subjective character of indexicality with the existence of quasi-logical truths involving indexicals.

There are also parallels in respect of the connexion between indexical logic and the unity of the subject: we can say that the holding of indexical logical truths is constitutive of what it is to be a single self. This is best seen by considering certain cases in which it might rashly be claimed that the usual indexical logic breaks down, namely split brain cases. Suppose it is held that in such cases we should speak of a single self composed of something like the (mereological) *sum* of the separated halves—a divided but unitary subject. Then it would appear permissible for one half to say, in respect of the other half, 'I am you', where the intended force of this is that the same person is knowingly presented to himself in these normally incompatible ways; for 'I' and 'you' will, on the view being considered, refer to one and the same (divided) subject.[28] Or again, if the two halves are spatially separated it might seem that 'I am here now' is no longer true, since it would be equally justified for each to say 'I am elsewhere now'—and these seem to be inconsistent assertions: that is, 'I am here now' could not be truly uttered with its usual force in the imagined circumstances. But

[28] More exactly, the usual rules of use for 'I' and 'you' would cease to hold in such a split brain case, since there would be no commitment to the distinctness of the referents of 'I' and 'you'; but this is to fly in the face of the very senses of those words.

surely the right conclusion is just that the abrogation of these logical truths is a *reductio ad absurdum* of the claim that a single self can be so divided: the word 'I' must be taken to refer to distinct selves as uttered by the results of a brain split, and for those selves the laws of indexical perspective hold in unmodified form.[29] Thus a single self cannot (knowingly) be presented with itself as both 'I' and 'you', or a place as 'here' and 'elsewhere': these modes of presentation exclude one another. So any case in which it might seem initially tempting to suppose that they are not thus incompatible is just a case in which we have to do with more than one subject; analogously to the way in which such a description is required for cases in which incompatible colours might seem a possibility for a perceptual subject.

The idea of a reduction to objective correlates also suggests itself for indexicals. Someone reluctant to acknowledge a special class of indexical logical truths, different in interpretation from logical truths involving non-indexical expressions, might suggest that a reduction of the former to the latter be carried out. The claim would be that we can explain the necessities discerned in indexical sentences in terms of non-indexical counterparts: we simply rewrite the indexical logical truths by replacing the indexical expressions with appropriate non-indexical expressions—rather as it was supposed that secondary quality logical truths could be reduced to primary quality logical truths. However, this attempt to eliminate a special class of indexical logical truths, and with it the thesis that these comprise laws of subjectivity, is easily shown to be impossible of fulfilment; for the corresponding non-indexical sentences will not preserve the logical truth of the originals. The reduction would proceed by replacing token indexicals with eternal expressions designating the same items—finding a 'translation' of each

---

[29] What I am doing here is giving edge to the compelling intuition that a brain split produces two distinct centres of consciousness: in effect, the logic of indexicals provides a criterion for counting subjects. Just as some initially tempting views of these split brain cases involve infringing the logic of identity, so (I am saying) other views involve infringing the logic of indexicals.

indexical utterance into an eternal sentence expressing (it is supposed) the same proposition. Now aside from the general problems attendant upon the feasibility of such a translation programme, this rewriting will not capture the logical status of the originals. First, we would lose the univocity of the original across different contexts or perspectives, since the tokens of the given indexical type will 'translate' into sentences with no semantic connexion of the kind induced by the indexical expressions: for example, 'I am not you' will dissolve into a heterogeneous list of sentences like 'John is not Jim', 'the first postmaster general is not the tallest man in Australia', etc. And second, the eternal counterparts do not preserve the epistemic status of their originals—in particular, they are not known *a priori*. I know the truth of the sentence 'I am here now' *a priori*, but I do not know *a priori* 'C.M. is in London on 15 November 1981'. It is also a necessary truth that the modes of presentation associated with the words in the indexical sentence should be related as the sentence asserts; but this is not true of the proffered non-indexical counterpart.[30] For these reasons, then, indexical logical truth must be regarded as *sui generis*. Indeed, the hopelessness of thus reducing indexical logic should reinforce the thesis that the presence of indexicality genuinely enriches the expressive power of a language: if indexical logic cannot be explained in terms of that which is not indexical, then indexical meaning will not be capturable by non-indexical meaning. In the same way, the difficulty of explaining the logic of secondary qualities in other terms constitutes a further argument for the irreducibility of secondary qualities to primary qualities. In both cases we have a system of elements conforming to laws which define those

---

[30] I have framed this necessity claim for 'I am here now' in such a way that it does not conflict with the correct point that a token of that sentence cannot be prefixed with 'necessarily'. The claim I am making is not that 'necessarily I am here now' expresses a truth when uttered, but rather that the modes of presentation associated with these indexical expressions necessarily yield a true thought when combined as that sentence combines them: concepts can necessarily yield a true thought without yielding a necessarily true thought.

elements; and the irreducibility of the laws goes hand in hand with the irreducibility of the elements.

The picture recommended by the considerations so far brought forward is as follows. In our perception of the world and in our thought about it the mind brings to bear a subjective contribution—of secondary qualities and indexical properties—which structure the way in which the world is mentally represented. These styles of representation exhibit a sort of logic, itself the upshot of the subjective constitution of the representing mind. We might say that in representing the world as having secondary qualities and indexical properties the mind imposes a subjective 'grid' upon its apprehension of things, a grid governed by its own internally determined principles and not reflective of what is objectively present in the world.[31] This raises the question, to be pursued in chapter 6, whether this subjective grid is a *necessary* feature of any conscious awareness of an external world, i.e. whether the subjective point of view, as thus exemplified, is ineliminable. When we have decided that question we shall be better able to assess the significance of the conclusions reached so far. But first we must fill out our account of what the two types of subjectivity involve by exposing some of their further distinctive characteristics.

[31] Perhaps I should warn that this denial of objectivity to secondary qualities is to be understood in a restricted sense, to be elaborated upon below: roughly speaking, I use 'objective' to mean 'mind-independent'. There are other notions of objectivity which secondary qualities fulfil, notably 'correctly predicated of non-mental objects'. As later sections will explain, I do not take the former denial of objectivity to entail denial of objectivity in the latter sense.

4
Incorrigible Identification

The claim that a certain type of property is subjective in nature raises the expectation that beliefs in respect of properties of that type are incorrigible. Thus the subjective nature of sensations such as pain shows in the fact that the subject's knowledge of his sensations is incorrigible: subjective states of affairs are detectable 'from the inside' and so their detection does not allow for error.[1] It is, of course, a substantive question why what has the property of subjectivity should also have the property of incorrigibility; but the connexion between the two notions makes it reasonable to enquire whether indexicals and secondary qualities have an incorrigibility property.[2] Indeed, it may be regarded as a condition of the truth of the claim that they are subjective that they are also incorrigible; and conversely, if they are incorrigible this may be taken as some confirmation of the subjectivity thesis, since incorrigibility is arguably a mark of the subjective. My twin questions are, then, these: is it true that a judgement that some item has an indexical property is incorrigible? and is it true that a judgement that some object has a secondary quality is incorrigible? Put differently, is it possible to misidentify the indexical properties and secondary qualities of things? I shall argue that the ascription of both is indeed incorrigible, thus satisfying the expectation

[1] In this chapter I follow the customary practice of using 'incorrigible' to mean 'infallible': I am interested in first-person immunity to error rather than the impossibility of being corrected by another or revising one's judgement at a later time.

[2] Insufficient attention has been paid to the question why what can be grasped only 'from the inside', i.e. by taking up a particular point of view, should also be infallibly known: why should the fact that there is something it is like to be in a particular state imply that the subject of the state has epistemological privileges with respect to it? Put differently, why should the *ontological* distinction between subjective and objective facts correlate with the *epistemological* distinction between infallibility and fallibility? The question seems to me to deserve exploration.

raised by the subjectivity theses and establishing a further point of similarity between indexicals and secondary qualities. However, the matter is not without complexity, especially as regards indexicals; careful formulation is needed if the incorrigibility is to be properly expressed.

There are, evidently, some judgements making indexical identifications which are incorrigible—in which no mistake resulting from a misidentification of some item as me, now, here, is possible. Thus consider 'I am in pain now' or 'I am thinking that I exist here': someone asserting these sentences could not be wrong about *which* items have the property thus attributed—the judger knows infallibly that it is himself here and now who is in pain or is thinking that he exists. This incorrigibility is not preserved when non-indexicals are substituted for indexicals, so as to get, for example, the judgement that C.M. is in pain in London on 16 November 1981; for I could easily be wrong that the person I know to be in pain is C.M. or that the time of the pain is 16 November or that the place is London. So the occurrence of indexicals is essential to the incorrigibility of self-ascriptions of psychological states—this is why Descartes must say 'I think' not 'Descartes thinks'.[3] Indexical identifications thus present their denotations in such a way that one cannot be mistaken about which items have the property in question. The intuitive difference between indexical and non-indexical identification is that the former does not attempt to venture beyond what is subjectively given, whereas the latter undertakes to locate the subject within objective coordinates.[4]

[3] The essential occurrence of indexicals in the *cogito* (and other incorrigible self-ascriptions) is not generally noted, but it is worth emphasising the point because it shows that the perspective from which a psychological state is ascribed is just as critical to the epistemological properties of the ascription as is the nature of the state ascribed: it is easy to neglect this point because we so naturally ascribe psychological states by means of indexicals. The fact is that there would be no incorrigible judgements without indexical modes of identification.

[4] Consider a total amnesiac: he does not know who he is, where he is, or when it is, but he has no trouble identifying these items indexically; he risks error only when he attempts to link those indexical identifications with the objective system of non-indexical identification.

My remarks about the impossibility of scepticism with respect to secondary qualities (chapter 2) already imply that the identification of the secondary qualities of a thing is incorrigible. The reason is that we know incorrigibly the kind of experience an object of perception produces, and on the dispositional analysis this *is* to know which secondary qualities the producing object has; the ascription of such experientially constituted qualities does not really require us to look beyond what is given 'from the inside' (which is not to say that these are not perceptible qualities of objects).[5] As I said earlier, this needs some qualification to make room for the distinction we customarily draw between real and apparent secondary qualities; but this does not seriously disturb the incorrigibility claim because it can either be made to apply at the level of the community or we can consider the simplified case of the solitary perceiver—the important point is just that the satisfaction conditions for secondary qualities are determined by features given from within experience. The ascription of primary qualities does not enjoy this kind of incorrigibility, since it is always logically possible that our experience should mislead us about the primary qualities an object possesses. As a consequence of this epistemological asymmetry, any attempt to reduce secondary qualities to a primary quality basis in the object— colour to wavelength and the like—will fail to preserve the incorrigibility of secondary quality ascriptions.[6] (Compare the replacement of indexicals by non-indexicals and the consequent loss of incorrigibility.)

The initial impression that indexicals afford incorrigible

[5] Cf. again Wittgenstein's pain patches (see note 5, chapter 2 above). I am here just assuming that 'sense-datum reports' are incorrigible: if you think they are not, the claimed asymmetry with primary qualities can survive in a weakened form, viz. that the only errors possible in the identification of secondary qualities are errors in one's beliefs about one's own experiences.

[6] I think, indeed, that the plausibility of this epistemological asymmetry itself casts doubt upon the reductionist theory: on Armstrong's view, being red is an unknown physical property of surfaces of which our experiences of looking red are merely a fallible sign (see *A Materialist Theory of the Mind*, pp. 270 f.). But surely it is inconceivable that we be totally wrong in our belief that there are red objects in the world (given that there are objects).

identifications might be supposed refuted by certain uses of
'I'. Wittgenstein distinguished two sorts of use to which 'I'
may be put: 'I' can be used 'as subject' or 'as object'.[7]
'I' is used as subject in 'I am in pain', 'I am trying to raise my
arm', and other self-ascriptions of psychological states; it
is used as object in 'I am bleeding', 'I have grown six inches',
and other self-ascriptions of bodily states. Wittgenstein
says that the as-subject uses do not allow for the possibility of
misidentification, whereas the as-object uses do allow for this
possibility. Following Shoemaker, let us say that when 'I'
is used as subject it is immune to error through misidentification, whereas it is not so immune when used as object.[8] We
have an error of identification involving 'I' when you know
of someone that he has a certain property and you mistakenly believe that person to be yourself: thus you can
know of someone that he is bleeding and wrongly think that
someone to be yourself; but you cannot know of someone
that he is in pain and wrongly take that someone to be yourself. In general, there are two possible sources of error in
any subject–predicate judgement, corresponding to the
predication component of the judgement and the identification component. In the case of 'I am bleeding' the mistake
can lie in the identification component, as well as in the
predication component; in 'I am in pain' it can lie in neither.
Corrigibility in the identification component can also occur
for the indexicals 'now' and 'here'. Suppose you are watching
some film of a battle which you take to be 'live coverage';
you may then come to know of a certain time that the battle
is occurring at that time, but mistakenly believe that time to
be now, and so judge, incorrectly, 'the battle is occurring
now'.[9] In similar circumstances, you could know it to be

---

[7] Wittgenstein, *The Blue and Brown Books*, pp. 66–7.

[8] Shoemaker, 'Self-Reference and Self-Awareness'.

[9] The logical form of this claim (and others of the same sort) is: '$\exists x$ (A knows
that Fx & A believes (falsely) that $x = i$)', where 'i' is some indexical. Where 'F'
is, e.g., 'in pain' and 'i' is 'I' the second conjunct cannot be true when the first is
true; where 'F' is, e.g., 'is six feet tall' the second conjunct can be true—the truth
of the identity belief is not in that case guaranteed.

raining at a certain place and mistakenly identify that place as here. It thus seems that indexical identifications are not *invariably* incorrigible: does this not undermine the incorrigibility thesis for indexicals and with it the subjectivity thesis? I shall argue that this conclusion is unwarranted.

In the first place, the incorrigibility of indexical identification in self-ascriptions of (certain) psychological states has not been cast into doubt; so it cannot be said that indexicals enjoy *no* epistemological privileges. But second, it is important to appreciate that as-object uses of 'I' are derivative or secondary uses, readily eliminable in favour of incorrigible as-subject uses.[10] When you mistakenly judge 'I am bleeding' you do so because you observe a certain body to be bleeding and you think that body is your own, perhaps because of its propinquity and similarity to your own body. What is primarily identified as a subject of predication here is a body, which is subsequently assigned to a certain self; so the object of *mis*identification is also in the first instance a body only. This is why it is natural to speak of as-object uses of 'I' as indirect or derivative. Indeed, as-object uses are always replaceable by 'my body', which brings out the fact that the object of reference about which the mistake is made is really something distinct from the self.[11] Moreover, as Shoemaker observes, the 'my' in 'my body' must be understood in its as-subject use: to say of a certain body that it is mine is to imply that it is the body through which I speak and act and which is the vehicle through which I undergo various sensations—and this is to use 'I' as subject and therefore incorrigibly.[12] All this could be put by saying that as-object uses of 'I' involve identifying oneself as the owner of a body which is itself identified by perceptual means, and this does

[10] Shoemaker argues convincingly for the priority of 'as subject' uses of 'I', op. cit., p. 567.

[11] What happens in as-object uses of 'I' is thus that (e.g.) an arm is mistakenly taken to be one's own; it is not really that one mistakenly takes another *self* to be one's own: there could not then be an *un*derivative misidentification of someone as oneself.

[12] Shoemaker, op. cit., p. 567.

not entail that the root use of 'I' is not as-subject. That there is this asymmetry in respect of corrigibility between the two uses no more compromises the subjectivity of 'I' than the epistemological asymmetry of 'pain' as between first- and third-person ascriptions compromises the subjectivity of pain sensations.[13] What holds for 'I' also holds for 'now' and 'here': the corrigible uses of these are derivative from and parasitic on incorrigible uses. The mistaken identifications mentioned above are based upon a supposed match between what is happening in the film and how things look to you here and now; and 'now' and 'here' occur incorrigibly in reports of how things look.[14] It seems to me, then, that the incorrigible use of indexicals is primary: we could not think or speak indexically unless there were incorrigible uses, and the corrigible uses are dependent upon the incorrigible uses.

I have written so far as if the identification component of a judgement could be incorrigible only if the predication component was—that is, 'I' is used as subject only in in-corrigible judgements. And this may make it seem strained to hold that as-subject uses are primary, as if 'I' is only properly used when self-ascribing subjective mental states. In fact, however, it seems that 'I' can be used as subject in certain corrigible judgements (as can 'now' and 'here') though we need to be careful about how these are delimited. The question here is whether there exist any corrigible judge-ments which are immune to error through misidentification, i.e. whose proneness to error derives exclusively from the predication component. Shoemaker suggests that 'I see a canary' and 'I am waving my arm' express such judgements: you can be wrong in making these judgements because you are hallucinating or paralysed, but you cannot be wrong (Shoemaker thinks) because you wrongly take yourself to

[13] Indeed, as-object uses of 'I' precisely involve taking a third-person perspec-tive on oneself—no wonder then that they are corrigible.

[14] That is, in order to be able to judge, on the basis of seeing a film, 'the battle is occurring now' or 'it is raining here' one has also to make judgements in which 'now' and 'here' occur incorrigibly—as in 'I am now/here watching a film of a battle/rain' or 'I now/here seem to be watching . . .'.

be the subject of the perceptions and actions you know to characterise someone else.[15] So stated, this suggestion appears incorrect. For suppose you are in the following position: it seems to you that you see a canary, and you see a reflection of someone in a mirror just like you who is looking at a canary; you would not normally trust your experience as of a canary to indicate that you are in fact seeing one (perhaps because you have been hallucinating a lot of canaries recently) but the mirror reflection provides adequate evidence, you suppose, that you are seeing a canary after all—so you boldly judge 'I see a canary'. But in point of fact the person reflected, who is seeing a canary, is not you and you are (as usual) hallucinating a canary. In this case you do know of someone that he sees a canary but you wrongly take that person to be yourself, and so judge incorrectly.[16] Or suppose you are trying to wave your arm while watching someone's arm waving: it may be that you believe correctly that someone is waving his arm, but wrongly judge 'I am waving my arm' because you mistake that person for yourself, on the reasonable ground that he looks just like you (etc.) and you are trying to wave your arm (but failing to). These out of the way cases show that the judgement *types* expressed by 'I see a canary' and 'I am waving my arm' are not immune to error through misidentification, since there are possible tokens of these types in which just such an error is committed. What does, however, seem true is that there also exist possible tokens of these types for which no such error can arise—namely, just those token judgements the sole ground for the assertion of which consists in the occurrence of a purely inner and subjective state: that is to say, judgements made on the basis of the truth of 'I *seem* to see a canary' and 'I am *trying* to wave my arm'. And of

---

[15] Shoemaker, op. cit., p. 557.
[16] This case can be described so as to avoid the assumption that you see the reflection of a canary and hence (arguably) do see a canary: perhaps the perceiver whose reflection you see wears an expression characteristic of looking at a canary, or perhaps you are reliably informed that the person reflected in the mirror is seeing a canary—in neither case do you see a reflected canary.

course in the usual case these *are* the grounds of the corresponding perceptual and action judgements; but these grounds are themselves incorrigible judgements. So it seems that 'I' is used as subject only in judgements asserted on the basis of incorrigible self-ascriptions of subjective states. The case of 'I am bleeding' is different in that it *cannot* be made on such a basis; it must always be grounded in perceptual observation of one's own or another's body.[17] We thus arrive at the following conclusions: first, that incorrigible indexical identification is not in fact confined to judgements which are incorrigible *simpliciter*; and second, that a close tie between indexical incorrigibility and the ascription of subjective states is nevertheless a fact to be acknowledged. This latter point reinforces the claim that the incorrigibility of indexicals does reflect an involvement in the subjective; the case is therefore not to be assimilated to the incorrigibility of (say) elementary arithmetic, where it would be wrong (or very contentious) to diagnose a subjective element. Indexicals and the self-ascription of subjective states are very intimately related.

The two uses of 'I' and their associated epistemological features have a certain parallel in the ascription of secondary qualities. I said before that such ascriptions are incorrigible; but this is to assume that the ascription is made upon an experiential basis, i.e. the conditions which define the ascribed secondary quality. Such direct experience is certainly the canonical basis for the ascription of secondary qualities, but we can imagine other sorts of basis for which incorrigible identification of secondary qualities will fail. Suppose you are examining the spectral reflection properties of a surface to which you have no direct visual access—in particular, you do not perceive its colour; and suppose you

---

[17] Of course, there is a sense in which 'I am bleeding' is asserted on the basis of the self-ascription of a subjective state, viz. 'I seem to be seeing a body that is bleeding': the difference from 'I see a canary' and 'I am waving my arm' is that, in cases in which 'I' is used incorrigibly in these judgements, the basis of identification of the person judged to have these properties does not go beyond an introspective report of a subjective state—in particular, there is no *perceptually* based identification of a person.

come to believe, correctly, that the colour of the surface is that associated with wavelength l (for normal human beings). However, you falsely believe that red is the colour associated with wavelength l, and hence judge that the surface is red. In fact, we can suppose, it looks green to normal human beings. In this case you have misidentified the colour of the surface. The case is like the case of 'I am bleeding' in that an objective basis is used for the identification, thus opening up the possibility of error: in both cases a non-canonical criterion of identification is employed—perception of a body and knowledge of a correlated wavelength—instead of the usual subjectively recognised basis of identification. In the colour case the derivative character of the criterion of identification is evident enough; and its availability would not make us doubt the essential subjectivity of colour. I suggested an analogous attitude toward the as-object uses of 'I'. In neither case is the possibility of corrigible identification a good reason to doubt the identification's essential and constitutive incorrigibility; so I think the intended contrast with non-indexical identification and the ascription of primary qualities survives the qualifications required by such derivative employments of indexicals and secondary quality words.

Let me conclude this section with two morals suggested by the above discussion. The peculiarities of 'I' in its as-subject use, specifically the impossibility of misidentification, have sometimes been thought to show either that 'I' does not refer at all or that its reference is a transcendental subject which eludes cognitive grasp.[18] And it has also been supposed that these peculiarities rule out any perceptual or

---

[18] Wittgenstein follows his discussion of immunity to error through misidentification by saying 'To say "I have pain" is no more a statement *about* a particular person than moaning is.' *The Blue and Brown Books*, p. 67. G. E. M. Anscombe likewise contends that 'I' is not a referring expression, and one of her reasons is the impossibility of misidentification: 'Getting hold of the wrong object *is* excluded, and that makes us think that getting hold of the right object is guaranteed. But the reason is that there is no getting hold of an object at all.' 'The First Person', p. 59. Shoemaker discusses the opposite tendency to make the self a transcendental object: 'Self-Reference and Self-Awareness', p. 560.

observational model of self-awareness.[19] The idea behind both of these suppositions is that it is a necessary condition of speaking of identification or recognition of an object that it be possible to *mis*identify or *mis*recognise the object— the thought being that identification involves the employment of a criterion, and that it ought to be possible to misapply the criterion. This sort of reasoning has made some philosophers say that sensations are not properly objects of identifying reference, and that it must be wrong to conceive our knowledge of them as based upon anything like observation of their presence.[20] In so far as these claims depend upon impossibilities of misidentification attendant upon the as-subject use of 'I', it seems that our earlier considerations undermine them. For, first, such misidentification is equally impossible for 'now' and 'here', yet no one would wish to hold that these do not refer to times and places or that their referents are transcendental.[21] And, second, it cannot be a necessary condition of a mode of awareness being perceptual that it permit the possibility of misidentification, since our awareness of secondary qualities is precisely perceptual even though there is not the kind of possibility of error required by the alleged necessary condition (this is clearest for the solitary perceiver).[22] So the fact that 'I' affords incorrigible identification, or indeed that 'pain' does, does not in itself imply that awareness of self and

[19] The general thesis that the property of infallibility is inconsistent with a perceptual account of the basis of the infallible judgement is, of course, a thesis of Wittgenstein's. Shoemaker, op. cit., wishes to derive a parallel lesson about self-awareness from the incorrigibility of as-subject uses of 'I'; but he does not want to maintain that 'I' is not designative.

[20] So Wittgenstein on the interpretation of sensation vocabulary.

[21] This point seems especially pressing for Anscombe; and it is significant that nowhere in 'The First Person' is any comparison made between 'I' and 'now' and 'here'. Note also that these indexicals provide an analogy for the security of 'I' against reference-failure (especially 'now').

[22] It would be misguided to try to resist this point by trading upon the *possibility* of a real-apparent distinction for secondary qualities; for such a distinction might be made for Wittgenstein's 'paininess' property and yet the basic incorrigibility of ascriptions of this property would not be thereby compromised. And then there is the fact that *community* ascriptions of secondary qualities are incorrigible though perceptually based.

awareness of pain are non-observational. (Not that I think these awarenesses are perceptual; I am just rejecting a certain argument for their not being perceptual.) What may, however, be true is that these cases of incorrigible identification are non-criterial: that is, they do not involve the application of some test which can conceivably fail to be satisfied. It seems that when we apply a name or definite description to some object, including our self, we do so on the strength of the presumed satisfaction of some criterion, and errors of identification arise when the object does not in fact satisfy the criterion. But when we apply 'I' it does not seem that we employ any such criterion of recognition—we just apply the word 'directly' and cannot be in error.[23] Similarly, our test for the instantiation of a primary quality is how things look or the results of measurement, and these may come apart from the primary qualities for which they test in a way that leads to error. But for secondary qualities we cannot really suppose our experience to constitute a test which may yield incorrect results; so the idea of employing a criterion seems out of place here. So if the application of a criterion is made to require the possibility of misapplication, then indexical words and secondary quality words are not (canonically) ascribed on the basis of criteria. But being criterionless in this sense is not a reason for supposing the basis of application not to be perceptual, still less a reason for denying the propriety of talk of identifying an object— 'incorrigible identification' is not a contradiction in terms.

---

[23] That is, in applying 'I' I do not, so to speak, cautiously hesitate until I am sure that a presented self meets some condition F which constitutes my criterion for 'I': I do not have to cast around among a number of candidates for 'I' for the one that satisfies such a criterial condition—if 'I' is being used as subject, that is.

5
Modes of Presentation

I have used the idea of an indexical mode of presentation in a fairly intuitive way, as the manner in which indexically identified items are represented in thought. It is time to enquire more closely into the structure of indexical modes of presentation, and in particular to ask how this type of mental representation relates to that which is represented. When we know in what manner indexicals represent the world we shall have a better idea of what a 'perspective' is, and so a clearer understanding of the form of the subjective point of view as it is expressed in the use of indexicals. Secondary qualities will come into the discussion towards the end.

In 'The Thought' Frege says 'everyone is presented to himself in a special and primitive way, in which he is presented to no-one else'; and he goes on to assert that no-one else *can* grasp thoughts which present the reference of 'I' in this special way.[1] So Frege's view is that I-thoughts are strictly incommunicable; and to say this is to say that they are subjective, in Frege's sense.[2] Now incommunicability has also been thought to attach to experience of secondary qualities: no-one else can ever grasp how you represent the world perceptually, at least in respect of colour, taste,

---

[1] Frege, 'The Thought: a Logical Inquiry', pp. 25–6.

[2] In 'On Sense and Reference' Frege gives as a reason for not identifying thoughts with ideas the (supposed) fact that ideas are subjective and incommunicable whereas thoughts are objective, public and shareable: see pp. 59–60. In 'The Thought' such an identification is rejected for the same kinds of reason (pp. 26 ff.), but Frege omits to mention that only a few pages earlier he has claimed the existence of private and unshareable thoughts. Perhaps his position is that the acknowledged publicity of *some* thoughts (those not involving 'I') cannot be respected by an identification with ideas: but still his general argument for postulating a 'third realm' of immaterial thoughts over and above mental states seems compromised by his claim about I-thoughts. (Note that combining Frege on 'I' with the Chisholm–Lewis thesis that all thoughts are *de se* has the consequence that *no* thoughts are communicable!)

etc.[3] The temptation to regard I-thoughts and secondary quality experience as incommunicable testifies to their subjectivity, but I do not think we should accept these incommunicability theses. Part of my purpose in this chapter is to criticise Frege's position on this question, while acknowledging the pressures which led him to it; for it is at least understandable why I-thoughts should be supposed incommunicable, bound up as they are with the special access one has to oneself. My other main aim is to elucidate the force of 'everyone is presented to himself in a special and primitive way' with a view to arriving at an account of the structure of modes of presentation. I begin with this latter question.

The very first thing to notice about the phrase in which we are interested is that it is ambiguous with respect to the scope of the quantifiers occurring in it, and that resolving the ambiguity is crucial to the whole question of the nature of indexical modes of presentation. Thus we can either assign wide scope to 'everyone' or to 'a special and primitive way', thereby obtaining the following two readings of Frege's words:

$\forall x \exists m (x$ is presented with x in m &
$\sim \Diamond \exists y (y$ is presented with x in m & $y \neq x))$

or

$\exists m \forall x (x$ is presented with x in m &
$\sim \Diamond \exists y (y$ is presented with x in m & $y \neq x))$

The difference, of course, is that the first reading allows that different people are presented to themselves in different ways, whereas the second claims that there is a single mode

---

[3] See Schlick, 'Form and Content', pp. 295 ff., and Bernard Harrison, *Form and Content*, esp. chap. 4. The incommunicability discussed by these writers relates to the alleged impossibility of *knowing* the content of another's experience; the Fregean notion of incommunicability is more a matter of the impossibility of *sharing* someone else's thought—I can know well enough that you are having an I-thought, but what I cannot do is grasp or share that very thought.

of presentation common to all people—they all think of themselves in the same way when they use 'I'. Let us label these two positions on the mode of presentation associated with 'I' the 'AE thesis' and the 'EA thesis', respectively. Note that the EA thesis is quite consistent with Frege's additional claim, expressed in the second conjunct, that no-one else can be presented with you as you are: they are indeed presented with *themselves* as you are presented with yourself, but this does not of course imply that they can be presented with *you* in that way—so sharing the 'I' mode of presentation does not entail the communicability of I-thoughts.[4] Note also that there is a suppressed time parameter in the above formulations which generates further readings of the original ambiguous phrase: should we strengthen the AE thesis to the claim that 'I' modes of presentation can vary over time by inserting '$\forall t$' between the initial quantifiers, or should we suppose a constant mode of presentation corresponding to each self over time? Similarly, should we strengthen the EA thesis by assuming a single mode of presentation constant over time, i.e. give '$\exists m$' wider scope than '$\forall t$', or should we say that the 'I' mode of presentation varies over time but is common to each person at any given time?[5] Given the general motivation behind the two views of the 'I' mode of

---

[4] Frege does not then *need* to recognise the existence of private unshareable modes of presentation in order to maintain the incommunicability thesis about 'I': it is rather that I cannot, in employing in my thought the mode of presentation you associate with your use of 'I', make *you* the referent of my thought—for when *I* employ that mode of presentation my referent necessarily becomes a distinct object, viz. myself. It is essential to this account of what is going on that the 'I' mode of presentation does not determine its reference-on-an-occasion: the complete Fregean thought would, on this view, be made up of a common shareable mode of presentation and an independently determined referent—instead of a private mode of presentation which sufficed to determine the referent.

[5] This latter alternative might be defended by suggesting, not altogether implausibly, that the 'now' mode of presentation is built into the 'I' mode of presentation, so that self-awareness is construed as inherently temporal. But to hold that the 'I' mode of presentation consequently varies over time is to assume that 'now' does not itself have a constant mode of presentation—which is really the same issue over again. We could allow the present time to enter the mode of presentation of a self at a time and still hold that this mode of presentation stays constant over time.

presentation, to be elaborated shortly, it would appear natural to adopt the strongest readings: the AE thesis allows for (or insists upon) the variation over time of each individual's unique mode of self-presentation, while the EA thesis claims that there is a constant such mode for any person and any time. However, nothing I say will turn upon accepting these strong readings; so it will do no harm to imagine the two theses relativised to a particular time. Two questions now arise: which reading did Frege intend? and which is the correct account of the 'I' mode of presentation?

As to Frege's intentions, I find nothing in what he says in 'The Thought' to permit any decisive disambiguation of the phrase in question: a reader of that work alone would not be able, I think, to discover whether Frege held the AE thesis or the EA thesis concerning the 'I' mode of presentation.[6] In view of the vast difference between the two theses this is somewhat surprising, but when we recall Frege's earlier theory of sense and reference it may come to seem less surprising—though less surprising in two opposed ways. On the one hand, it might be suggested that Frege is simply assuming, correctly or incorrectly, that the classical theory of sense and reference carries over to indexicals like 'I'; and it is an axiom of this theory that sense (= mode of presentation) determines reference, thus ruling out EA and embracing AE.[7] On the other hand, it might be said that Frege is here inchoately aware of the problems posed by indexicals for this earlier doctrine of sense and reference—in particular, for the principle that sense determines reference—and is accordingly equivocating on which interpretation of indexical modes of presentation he wishes to adopt.[8] It is probably futile to try to settle this exegetical dispute, and it is certainly not within

---

[6] *Pace* Chisholm, who simply assumes that Frege held what I am calling the AE thesis: see *The First Person*, p. 16.

[7] This would appear to be the view of Gareth Evans, 'Understanding Demonstratives'.

[8] We would then be using John Perry's view, in 'Frege on Demonstratives', to explain the ambiguity of Frege's statement—that he was caught between the truth about indexicals and fidelity to his earlier theory of sense and reference.

my brief to do so: my only comment is that it is by no means obvious that Frege held the AE thesis in 'The Thought'. And I have an additional reason for supposing that he did not hold it, namely that it seems to me an extremely implausible view. In short, Frege must either abandon a key principle of his earlier theory of sense and reference or commit himself to an implausible view of the sense of 'I'.[9] It is interesting to compare Frege's remarks with those of Husserl who is quite unambiguously an AE theorist. Husserl says: 'The word "I" names a different person from case to case, and does so by way of an ever altering meaning'; and again: 'Each man has his own 'I-presentation (and with it his individual notion of I) and this is why the word's meaning differs from person to person'.[10] Husserl takes a parallel position on the other indexicals, where again the choice between an AE or an EA thesis arises: do 'now' and 'here', for example, carry a single constant mode of presentation from occasion to occasion, or is it that there are different such modes for each different occasion? Before I give my reasons for favouring the EA thesis, let me make some remarks about the second conjunct of my formulation of Frege's comments on 'I' in relation to the other indexicals.

Frege says that I cannot be presented with you as you are presented to yourself; but he does not say analogous things about 'now' and 'here'. He does not say that each time/place is presented at that time/place in a special and primitive way, in which it is not (and cannot be) presented at other times/places: that is, he does not suggest that thoughts expressed with 'now' and 'here' are accessible only to thinkers who can apply 'now' and 'here' to the objects of such thoughts, as he does for 'I'. Indeed, he says things which are directly inconsistent with such a view; for he allows that the very same

[9] Dummett's view is that indexicals force Frege to separate out two distinct strands in his notion of sense: sense as linguistic significance, and sense as mode of presentation: see *The Interpretation of Frege's Philosophy*, chap. 6. He does not entertain the possibility that the mode of presentation might simply follow the linguistic significance, thus yielding the EA thesis.

[10] Husserl, *Logical Investigations*, pp. 315–16.

thought I express today with 'Today it is cold' can be expressed tomorrow with 'Yesterday it was cold', and similarly
for 'here' and 'there'.[11] In other words, granted the equation
of sense with mode of presentation, Frege holds that a given
time or place can be presented in the same way to thinkers
at different times or places, but he denies that the same self
can be presented in the same way to different selves. The
question is why he took a different view of 'I' and the other
indexicals in this respect: why is it that I can now grasp the
thought you expressed yesterday with 'Today it's cold' and
I can here grasp the thought you express from over there
with 'Here it is windy', but I cannot grasp the thought you
express when you say 'I am wounded'? It cannot be said that
Frege offers any answer to this rather natural question, and
I think that a comparison between 'I' and the other indexicals casts doubt upon his thesis of the incommunicability of
I-thoughts. He does say that I do not express the thought
Dr Lauben expresses when he says 'I am wounded' if I say
'Dr Lauben is wounded'; but this hardly establishes any
asymmetry with the other indexicals, since (as Frege would
surely agree) I do not express by 'On 17 November 1981 it
was cold' the same thought as I express today by saying
'Today it is cold', despite the identity of the days. Clearly,
we will need to employ an appropriate *indexical* expression if we are to express in another context the thought
expressed in an utterance employing a corresponding
indexical. What is curious is that Frege does not discuss the
obvious candidate for this corresponding indexical in the case
of 'I', namely 'you' (or perhaps 'he'): can I not express
Dr Lauben's thought by saying 'you are wounded' (or 'he is
wounded')? On the face of it, 'I' and 'you' are related in just
the way 'yesterday' and 'today' are, or 'here' and 'there'.
It may be replied that allowing a token of 'I' to have the
same sense as a token of 'you' puts the notion of a mode of
presentation under considerable strain: for how can it be
maintained that my presentation of myself when I use 'I' is

[11] See 'The Thought', p. 24.

identical with your presentation of me when you use 'you' of me—surely *these* are distinct ways of thinking of an object if any are? This is a forceful enough point, but it also seems to apply equally to the other indexicals: surely the ways of thinking correlated with different tenses are different, yet Frege holds them to be capable of expressing the same mode of presentation. Similarly, the way I apprehend a place when I think of it as 'here' seems very different from the way you do when you think of the same place as 'there' (suppose we are in different galaxies). In all these cases the idea of a constant cross-contextual mode of presentation is put under a good deal of pressure: the question is why, for Frege, the cross-contextual connexions between modes of presentation snap only in the case of 'I' and 'you'. It looks as if we should either hold that mode of presentation cannot be preserved across contexts in *all* cases or that it can be preserved in the case of 'I'. It is indeed a difficult question which option to take; my point is just that, for all anything Frege says, the decision should be made uniformly. The only ground of distinction I can surmise (a ground with no textual evidence) is that Frege believes that I cannot really be *presented* with Dr Lauben's self at all but only (say) with his body. The reference of 'I' would then be inaccessible from a third-person perspective in much the way that a person's mental states have often been supposed to be. Suppose I say to someone 'this pain is terrible' and he wishes to express my thought: it might be said that he cannot really do so, since he cannot really be presented with my pain itself but only with its behavioural symptoms. Put somewhat less strongly, the doctrine is that our ways of thinking of my pain are so different, on account of the epistemological asymmetry between first- and third-person knowledge, that we cannot think one and the same thought concerning a particular sensation. Perhaps Frege was moved by such doctrines in respect of 'I'; he was presupposing a radical epistemological difference between first- and third-person perspectives on a mental life.[12] This would certainly distinguish the case of 'I' from the other indexicals, but it imports an element into Frege's philosophical thinking whose presence had not been signalled before. It would be somewhat surprising to find such a Cartesian sentiment behind Frege's views on 'I'; but it seems to be the only way of explaining his divided treatment of indexicals.

The EA thesis asserts that, in any thought whose verbal expression contains a given indexical, the reference of that indexical is conceptualised in the same way: when someone has a thought corresponding to 'I am cold', the way he conceives of the reference of 'I' is the same as the way someone else conceives of himself in having such a thought; and similarly for 'now', 'here' etc. If we regard thoughts as complexes of concepts, then the EA thesis says that the concept corresponding to an indexical word type is the same for any token of that type. The equation of mode of presentation and concept underlines the point that a mode of presentation (a sense) is to correspond with what is in the mind of a thinker by way of a representation of the object of his thought; hence it is to constitute what Frege calls cognitive significance. What recommends the thesis that indexical concepts are thus constant? The first and fundamental consideration is the constancy of the linguistic meaning of indexicals from occasion to occasion. No theory of sense which entails denying this semantic constancy can be correct, and any theory which acknowledges it is compelled to discern a parallel constancy at the level of thought, since thoughts must have common conceptual elements if their

[12] We might put the point this way: Frege is assuming that the epistemological barrier between first-person thought and third-person understanding of such thought is impenetrable in a way that the gap between present-time thoughts and their subsequent understanding is not (similarly this-place thoughts and their comprehension from other places). For memory puts us into cognitive contact with earlier times, and perception makes us acquainted with other places; but (the Cartesian claim goes) no comparable faculty puts us on to the self of another or his inner states. If such Cartesianism is ultimately what is behind Frege's incommunicability thesis about 'I', then Perry is wrong to diagnose *this* thesis as arising from *general* problems that indexicals pose for Frege's theory of sense and reference: see 'Frege on Demonstratives'.

linguistic expression does. It is utterly different with proper names and definite descriptions: they cannot have different denotations without a difference of meaning, and so thoughts expressible with these words cannot be equivalent to thoughts expressible using indexicals. The EA thesis about indexical modes of presentation thus perfectly comports with their linguistic meaning, whereas the AE thesis is forced either to deny the constancy of linguistic meaning or to sever the tie between the structure of thoughts and the structure of sentence meaning.[13] The naive view suggested by indexical word meaning is thus that in thinking of items under 'I', 'now', 'here' one applies a single constant concept—the concept of oneself, of the present, and of the spatial vicinity— and not variable occasion-relative concepts.

A second consideration draws attention to certain constitutive connexions between modes of presentation and action. Presumably the Fregean notion of cognitive significance of an expression determines its cognitive role, and this in turn determines the person's dispositions to action— for example, which sentences he is prepared to assert under what conditions. Granted this connexion between thought content and action, it appears reasonable to individuate modes of presentation according to the dispositions to action with which they correlate—same dispositions, same mode of presentation. And as a number of writers have observed, dispositions to action induced by indexical thoughts correspond with the linguistic meaning of the associated indexical sentence: you and I are disposed to act in the same way if we both think 'I am about to be attacked by a bear' (other things being equal).[14] Similarly, 'now' has a constant cognitive role in practical reasoning eventuating in action. The EA thesis explains this, while the AE thesis must regard it as

[13] We find Husserl (op. cit., p. 316) denying this constancy but at the same time uneasy about declaring indexicals to be 'equivocal expressions': the result is no clear answer to the question what is the conceptual content of an indexical thought.

[14] See esp. Perry, 'The Problem of the Essential Indexical'. I am in general agreement with Perry and indebted to his treatment of these matters.

anomalous. None of this is to say—what is patently untrue
—that different thinkers employing indexical concepts do
not commonly associate distinct bodies of information with
their indexically identified objects of thought: that is, I am
not saying that you and I have the same *conception* of
ourselves, in the sense that we associate the same information
with our respective uses of 'I'. Neither am I saying that suc-
cessive times identified as 'now' are cognitively indistinguishable for the temporal thinker; and similarly for 'here'. My
claim rather concerns the conceptual content directly expressed by indexicals, not other associated beliefs a person
may have about his objects of reference. We need here the
distinction, familiar from discussions of the sense of proper
names, between the strict sense of the expression and the
collateral information a person may associate with it: you
and I may well (I trust do) associate different bodies of information with our respective uses of 'I', but it does not
follow that 'I' expresses a different individual concept in our
respective mouths (or minds). If this be doubted, we can
always correct for the intrusion of variable collateral information by imagining two persons whose self-descriptions are
identical but whose I-thoughts concern distinct objects:
and then the coincidence of their dispositions to action will
be obvious.

This last point suggests a further way of demonstrating the
EA thesis: we imagine cases in which the conceptual contents
of two minds, or of one mind at different times and places, is
held fixed while the objects of indexical thought are seen to
vary. Typically, when we travel through space, for example,
thinking of different places as 'here', the perceived scene
varies; and different concepts are brought to bear upon the
perceived environment. But suppose we meddle with someone's sensory input in such a way as to make it invariant as
the person is moved through space: then it seems that the
world will be presented to him in the same way as he moves
from place to place, the same concepts applied, but he nevertheless thinks of *different* places when he thinks 'here it is

cold'. And a similar story could be told about 'now'. According to the AE thesis, it should not be possible for minds of the same conceptual content to take different objects of thought; but it should now be clear that this is no more acceptable than the idea that one cannot refer to distinct objects by using an expression with a constant linguistic meaning. The *context* of thought or utterance is what ties the indexical mode of presentation down to particular things, not the concepts in the mind of the thinker; so these latter can stay constant while what is thought about varies.[15]

A final reason for favouring the EA thesis is that it helps to explain why indexicality is irreducible. Husserl's advocacy of the AE thesis leads him to suggest, as conformable with that thesis, the in-principle reducibility of indexical meaning to non-indexical meaning; for the meaning of 'I' varies from use to use as a function of the variations in what is true of its denotation, and Husserl naturally supposes that we could therefore replace 'I' with those variably true descriptions.[16] His picture is that each person has a number of descriptive beliefs about himself which constitute his self-conception; so, since these determine the meaning of 'I' on an occasion, it ought to be possible to eliminate 'I' in favour of those descriptions. And he holds something analogous about the other indexicals. It thus seems that the AE thesis, motivated in the way Husserl motivates it, leads naturally to the idea that indexical meaning is not semantically fundamental, that it does not really contribute to the expressive power of a

[15] It should also be evident enough that these concepts in no way 'contain' their referent and do not depend for their existence upon it—just as the linguistic meaning of an indexical is independent of the existence (and identity) of its denotation. But note that this is *not* to say that complete indexical thoughts (i.e. truth-evaluable propositions) are likewise existentially independent of reference; for they incorporate, in addition to indexical concepts, contextually determined references. See my paper 'The Structure of Content' for more on this duplex conception of propositions.

[16] Husserl writes: 'The content meant by the subjective [indexical] expression, with sense oriented to the occasion, is an ideal unit of meaning in precisely the same sense as the content of a fixed [non-indexical] expression. This is shown by the fact that, ideally speaking, each subjective expression is replaceable by an objective expression which will preserve the identity of each momentary meaning-intention.' op. cit., p. 321.

language. But the EA thesis strongly suggests that indexicality is semantically irreducible, because the constant conceptual element will not be capturable by means of definite descriptions and proper names, these being variable in meaning across different referents. Since the irreducibility of indexicality is a desirable consequence of a theory of indexical modes of presentation, it seems that the EA thesis has the advantage over the AE thesis. (These remarks are not intended as *proof* that the AE thesis entails reducibility while the EA thesis entails irreducibility; they are intended merely to be suggestive. We would need to know a lot more about the detailed form of an AE theory, and about the ground of the irreducibility of indexicality, before the matter could be settled conclusively.)

My conclusion, then, is that the concept expressed by a given token of 'I' or 'now' or 'here' is the same as that expressed by other tokens of those types; which is to say that the mode of presentation and hence cognitive significance associated with different tokens of a given indexical (type) expression is constant. This entails giving up the classical Fregean theory of sense and reference, if sense is understood to comprise the conceptual content of a thought, i.e. what cognitively transpires in the mind of the thinker.[17] Putting this result together with our earlier conclusions about indexical representation, we have the thesis that the

---

[17] I find Evan's position in 'Understanding Demonstratives' crucially unclear on this point. He tells us that the sense of a (token) indexical is to be understood as whatever relation it is that makes a certain object the reference of that indexical then: but the question is whether such a sense can be construed as a *conceptual content* or whether appeal must be made to extra-conceptual (i.e. contextual) factors. The thrust of the Perry position, which Evans takes himself to be criticising, is precisely that indexical thoughts differ from descriptive thoughts inasmuch as conceptual content determines reference in the latter case but not in the former. Unless the issue is seen in this light, the dispute between supporters and critics of Frege will degenerate into an uninteresting verbal quarrel about the word 'sense'. An anticipation of the Perry view of indexical thoughts, which helps illuminate its purport, is to be found in P. T. Geach, *Mental Acts*, pp. 63–4, where Geach says that particular judgements expressed by means of the same indexical sentence (type) in different contexts have the same 'intelligible content' and that there is 'no difference to be found on the side of the judgement itself'.

subjective grid imposed by indexical thought has an EA structure: the mind applies a constant subjective perspective to the world. It seems to me that these two properties of indexical representation—subjectivity and constancy—are not just accidentally found together: in particular, constancy is not surprising in the light of subjectivity. For if the indexical perspective is something imposed by the mind, we might expect that its internal structure not be answerable to variations in how the world objectively is. I might put the point in terms of direction of fit: if a kind of representation has a subjective source, then it is not required that it fit what is objectively and antecedently present in the world; and this means that it is not required to conform its representations to objective differences between things. One might think it a fault in a system of representation that it employs a single mode of representation for indefinitely many things represented; but if the representational system is not intended to reflect objective differences, but rather to bring things within a subjective point of view, then this will not look like a defect. Things can be brought into relation to a subjective perspective by means of a constant manner of conception. Since a subjective system of representation does not *purport* to fit what is objectively the case, it can be oblivious in its structure to objectively drawn distinctions. (This thought should become clearer when we come to consider the structure of secondary quality perception.)

I have now attributed three properties to the indexical perspective: it is subjective, incorrigible and constant. Other writers have claimed that indexicality plays a special role in practical reasoning. Thus Casteñeda teaches us that the content of an intention always contains a self-reference: an agent intends that *he* shall do such-and-such, where the 'he' here must correspond to a first-person use of 'I' (indeed an as-subject use)—to intend something necessarily involves being aware of oneself as agent under 'I'.[18] And Perry argues that practical reasoning must involve beliefs in the content

[18] See H.-N. Casteñeda, *Thinking and Doing*, chap. 6.

of which indexical concepts occur ineliminably: I will not take appropriate action when about to be run over by a car unless I believe that *I* am about to be run over by a car *now*; and I will not terminate a journey to Oxford unless I believe 'Oxford is *here*'.[19] These indexical beliefs change one's informational state in a way that is essential to action. I agree with these writers that indexical attitudes are integral to agency, so that one who lacked indexical concepts could not have the propositional attitudes necessary to intentional action. Putting this together with the other properties I have attributed to the indexical perspective, then, we arrive at the idea that agency requires possession of a subjective point of view which has the EA structure and which permits incorrigible identification.[20] (What we lose in objectivity by having indexical thoughts we gain in powers of action.) As a consequence, we can say that the constancy of indexical representation is integral to agency: modes of presentation conforming to the classical theory of sense and reference—those with an AE structure—are not adequate to the requirements of an agent. These several interrelated features of the indexical perspective invite an investigation of the basis of their connexion —some kind of theory of *why* the notions of agency, incorrigibility, subjectivity and constancy go together. But providing such a unifying theory seems to me a very difficult task, and I am unable to offer any very illuminating account of the matter; I merely record the interrelations and note their significance. A natural next question would be whether *theoretical* reasoning can get by without indexical concepts, and hence without a subjective view and all that goes with it; or is there something *distinctive* about the necessity to act which requires possession of a subjective point of view?[21]

---

[19] Perry, 'The Problem of the Essential Indexical'.

[20] This appears to have theological consequences: if God is an agent, then He must have a subjective indexical point of view on space and time; but this requires that He be *in* space and time, since indexical thoughts are interpreted only by occurring in a spatio-temporal context.

[21] It is surely no accident that indexicals have most often been supposed dispensable in areas of theoretical reasoning such as physics and mathematics.

I shall touch on this question later, having noted its relevance to the question of the connexions between the cited features of indexical modes of presentation.

I made it a constraint upon any theory of indexical modes of presentation that the constant linguistic meaning of indexical expressions be respected; and I suggested that this constraint blocks certain reductionist views about indexical meaning. Do these points have any parallel in the case of secondary qualities? It may seem unlikely that they should, but I think it is worth indicating a certain point of analogy. Keith Campbell suggests as a constraint upon theories of the significance of colour words that they should assign a single colour property to each (unambiguous) colour word: he calls this the 'axiom of unity', and he observes that certain theories of colour violate it.[22] Thus theories which try to reduce colours to underlying physical properties are in danger of violating the axiom of unity because of the demonstrable variability of the underlying physical properties; colour words are not univocal according to those theories. Such reductionist theories even go so far as to suggest that colour properties are not genuine properties at all if they cannot be reconstructed at the primary quality level. In other words, colour terms are being treated as natural kind terms, for which an axiom of unity would be inappropriate, since we want to allow that we may have picked out distinct natural kinds despite their superficial resemblance.[23] But in the case of secondary qualities like colour the axiom of unity seems a potent force against reductionist proposals; it has the same kind of force as the requirement that (intuitively unambiguous) sensation words should designate the same kind of sensation according to any good theory of mental states.[24] The point of analogy with indexicals should now be

[22] Campbell, 'Colours', pp. 132-3.
[23] As with Putnam's 'jade' case: see 'The Meaning of "Meaning" ', p. 241. By contrast, we do not want to allow that 'red' or 'sweet' may be *ambiguous*.
[24] That is, we have no inclination to say that 'pain' is as many ways ambiguous as there are different physical realisations of that sensation: see my 'Mental States, Natural Kinds and Psychophysical Laws'. As will have become apparent,

plain: the axiom of unity in respect of secondary qualities plays a similar anti-reductive role to that of the EA thesis in respect of indexicals—both requirements insist upon the reality of groupings which cannot be captured in primary quality terms or in non-indexical terms. Nor is the analogy altogether fortuitous, I think. The classifications effected by secondary quality words differ in *point* from those effected by natural kind words, and so differ with respect to what is to count as a defective system of classification. With natural kinds, whose characterisation proceeds in primary quality terms, the system of classification must be responsible to how things objectively are—the classification must *fit* the objective world; but secondary quality classifications do not purport to fit what is objectively present in the world independently of experience, and so cannot be criticised for failing to conform to classifications arrived at on objective grounds—their role is rather to classify objects by way of their sensory appearance. So it is the subjective source of secondary qualities which makes the axiom of unity reasonable—that is, which frees secondary quality classifications from the obligation to fit the objective condition of the world. To put it in a way that brings out the analogy: the subjectivity of secondary qualities lies behind their constancy *vis-à-vis* underlying primary qualities, rather as the subjectively based imposition of an indexical perspective can be seen to lie behind its EA structure: in neither case is it a matter of a system of representation whose obligation it is to fit the world in its objective nature. The idea of a subjective grid contributed by the mind is the operative consideration in both cases.

issues about the semantics of secondary quality words and sensation words are remarkably parallel, which is unsurprising given that the latter enter into the analysis of the former.

6
On the Ineliminability
of the Subjective View

When an aspect of our means of representing the world has been shown to have a subjective source it is natural to ask whether that aspect is eliminable. The thought is that if a way in which things are represented is contributed by the mind it ought to be possible to envisage a form of mental representation in which this subjective contribution is absent, a form which is purely objective in its representational content. An obvious example of this is perceptual illusions: the world is perceived in a certain way because of the distorting effects of the sensory system, and so we get the idea of a form of perception which is not subject to these subjective intrusions. Or consider vagueness: suppose we decided (rightly or wrongly) that the occurrence of vague concepts in our thought arose, not from any objective vagueness in the world, but from features of our own powers of representation. We might then envisage the elimination of these vague concepts from our thought, leaving only precise and thus objective concepts; or if not an extrusion of vagueness from our own thought, then a conception of a being whose thought is *ab initio* innocent of vague concepts—God, as we might suppose. The motive for such elimination would be to represent things as they are in themselves, not as they strike a mind which injects its own peculiarities into its representation of the world.[1] The position I have been developing about secondary qualities and indexicals invites this sort of question in their regard: can we form a conception of a type of mind whose representations are free of secondary quality perceptions and

---

[1] We might, familiarly, take this as a programme of conceptual purification: the ideal system of representation is conceived as entirely objective in content, and it is a philosophical desideratum to approach this ideal by isolating and expelling subjective elements. I shall be discussing the credentials and prospects of such a programme of purification.

indexical modes of presentation? To ask this is not, of course, to ask whether a description of how our minds *actually* are need make ineliminable mention of secondary quality experience and indexical concepts; the question is whether there could be a mind which simply lacked these subjective features—a purely objective mind.[2] The focus of my interest in broaching this question is the case of secondary qualities, though I think indexicals raise parallel questions which help clarify the issues. The question, then, is whether, and if so why, the ascription of secondary qualities to objects of experience and thought is ineliminable; and this is the question whether the subjective view as embodied in the perception of secondary qualities is dispensable. I have argued that the subjective view exists and is irreducible; I am now asking whether its existence is necessary or contingent. And clearly the significance of the former claim depends upon the answer we give to the latter question.

The issue of elimination arises at two points: in relation to our *concepts* of external things, and in relation to our *percepts* of external things. We must ask, then, whether we (or some other being) can (could) *conceive* of physical objects as possessing primary but not secondary qualities; and whether perceptual *experience* can be as of only primary qualities: that is, whether these two cognitive faculties can represent things just as they are in themselves.[3] Now the thesis that we can form an absolute conception of things *requires* that secondary qualities be thus eliminable from our picture of the world, these being credited to the perceiver's subjective

---

[2] My question is thus not the same as Nagel's in 'Subjective and Objective' and elsewhere: his question is whether subjective properties can be accommodated within an objective conception of the world—in particular, whether we can give an objective characterisation of mental states; my question is rather whether we can make sense of a representing mind which does not ascribe subjectively constituted features to the (external) world.

[3] This can be put as a question about the necessary conditions of intentional content with respect to propositional attitudes and perceptual experience: must any thought whose content includes a primary quality concept also include a secondary quality concept (or more weakly, be necessarily associated with thoughts incorporating such concepts)? and must the content of experience represent objects as having secondary qualities if it represents them as having primary qualities? (If the two questions received different answers, then clearly we would need different accounts of the two kinds of intentional content.)

peculiarities.[4] I shall later enquire what sort of representation can fulfil the conditions for being a purely objective
and absolute conception of the world; my present concern is
more with the eliminability of secondary qualities from
perception. (This is in fact the prior question, since the
question of the nature of the absolute conception must turn
upon whether it is explicable in perceptual terms: if secondary
qualities are ineliminable from perception, then it seems that
the absolute conception cannot be given content by recourse
to a special form of perception of a kind we only contingently
lack.) Perceptual experience which represented the world
only in terms of primary qualities would have an entirely
objective content; the world would not be perceived to have
qualities which depend upon the perceiver's specific sensory
make-up. Is this intelligible? The analogous question about
indexicals is whether we can make sense of a form of direct
cognitive awareness of space, time and ourselves which does
not involve thinking of these items under indexical modes of
presentation. The judgements in the making of which we
enjoy direct cognitive contact with things in the world typically involve indexical concepts; but is this a *necessary* truth
about such direct cognitive awareness?[5] Can we envisage a
mind which has the faculty of direct cognitive awareness, but
which lacks indexical thoughts? Note that I am not here
asking whether there could be a thinking being who lacked
perception of secondary qualities and indexical concepts; I
am asking the more limited question whether a being *capable
of perception and of direct cognitive awareness* could sustain these lacks—and it may be that we can make sense of a
mind which does not have *those* faculties. Of course, if
we decided that such a purely ratiocinative mind was impossible, then my more limited question would have a greater

---

[4] See Williams, *Descartes*, pp. 241-7.

[5] By this I mean something like Russell's notion of acquaintance: see
Problems of Philosophy, chap. 5. Put in these terms, the question is whether the
relation of acquaintance must always be mediated by indexical concepts. (We
might see Russell's sometime claim that 'this' is the only genuine proper name as
(in part) an expression of an affirmative answer to this question.)

significance than I am claiming for it; but I will not undertake any demonstration of the stronger claim here.[6]

Let us first set out some *prima facie* reasons for supposing the elimination of secondary quality experience to be possible in principle. Some of these alleged reasons seem to me to be based on mistakes, though intelligible and interesting mistakes; others start from correct premises which give initially appealing grounds for expecting elimination to be possible. It is not that I think any of these reasons constitutes a successful argument for eliminability; my purpose in setting them out is to heighten our sense of the significance of the claim of *in*eliminability—I want to show that it is not philosophically trivial to insist upon this ineliminability thesis.

There are those who hold that it is a kind of perceptual illusion to perceive secondary qualities as instantiated by external things: in point of fact, it is thought, secondary qualities are instantiated by items which are strictly 'in the mind'—but we are prone to 'objectify' them. In projecting secondary qualities from the mind to the world our perceptual apparatus thus commits us to an *error* concerning their true location.[7] Now, as I shall later argue, I do not think an error theory of our perception of secondary qualities is

---

[6] In assessing this stronger thesis we should need to distinguish two questions: whether there could be a mind capable of learning about the empirical world which lacked perceptual experience of its denizens; and whether there could be a mind whose thoughts were limited to subject-matters for which perceptual experience is inappropriate, e.g. mathematics. The conceptual impossibility of the former case would seem easier to establish than that of the latter case: if it were established, then our question could be expanded to 'must any being with knowledge of the empirical world experience it as instantiating secondary qualities?' But I won't try to make out this connexion between empirical knowledge and perceptual experience here, though I believe it could be done. The analogous question about indexicals is whether there could be a mind whose knowledge of the world was exclusively descriptive, i.e. a mind which never stood in the relation of acquaintance to anything. Again, I believe the impossibility of this could be established, thus enlarging the scope of my question about the eliminability of indexical concepts; but I shall refrain from embarking upon a defence of this claim here.

[7] This seems to be J. L. Mackie's view, *Problems from Locke*, chap. 1. Locke himself can be read as holding such an 'error theory': see his *Essay*, II, viii, 24–5. What is not wholly clear to me is whether these authors take the error to be perceptual or judgemental or both: I think they suppose that perceptual experience

acceptable; my present point is that one who holds such a theory has every reason to expect their eliminability from experience—and indeed those philosophers inclined to an error theory tend also to favour the idea of elimination. For it is very natural to hold that all errror is in principle remediable: to have the idea of a certain kind of error is to have the idea of what would count as a rectification of the error—and in this case it would be perception without secondary qualities. An error theorist *might* say that the error is logically inescapable, that not even God's perceptions are free of it; but, given his theory, this seems forced—better not to violate the principle that all error is remediable. At any rate, the error theory motivates a claim of eliminability, though it may not actually entail it.

A somewhat less extreme motive for expecting eliminability might come from the idea that our perception of secondary qualities involves, not error, but ignorance: we perceive colours, say, because our senses are not acute enough to allow us to perceive surfaces in the way science describes them (Locke's texture of imperceptible parts).[8] Indexicals provide a good analogy for this type of view: it has often been held that we use indexicals simply because we are ignorant of the non-indexical descriptions of things.[9] Someone who holds this sort of view of secondary qualities—as reductionists about colour by implication do—will naturally suppose that there could be a form of perception for which

invites an error of judgement, though to say our perception of colour literally involves a visual *illusion* would be a bit too much.

[8] Thus Reid says that the 'notions of the vulgar' as to the nature of secondary qualities 'are confused and indistinct, rather than erroneous'. *Essays on the Intellectual Powers of Man*, p. 258. His view that a secondary quality like colour 'is an unknown cause or occasion of well known effect' (loc. cit.) is strikingly similar to Armstrong's view in *A Materialist Theory of the Mind*, chap. 12.

[9] Strawson's discussion in *Individuals*, chap. 1, of the role of demonstrative identification in solving the putative problem of 'reduplication' might suggest such a conception of indexical expressions: omniscient speakers and hearers would have no real use for demonstrative identification. (I do not say that Strawson explicitly asserts this; only that it is a natural construction to put on the general direction of his discussion.)

this ignorance is remedied; for to eliminate secondary qualities from perception will just be to make up for a contingent state of ignorance. Again, it might be said that the ignorance is incurable; but this would be something surprising given the original theory—as surprising as the absolute ineliminability of indexicals on an ignorance theory of them.

A different sort of rationale for eliminability depends upon the idea that perception ought to recapitulate conception: perceptual content ought, in principle, to be capable of mirroring how we conceive the world.[10] Now it seems possible to form the idea of an object all of whose properties are causally efficacious; this is indeed what a scientific description aims at—a scientific conception of objects eliminates all that is theoretically otiose. But then why should perception not be answerable to, and capable of fulfilling, the same requirement: that its representational content not exceed what is causally efficacious? It would seem, from this point of view, somewhat surprising if perceptual content *could* not satisfy this principle of parsimony. Consider the case of God. On the face of it, it seems consistent to suppose both that God can perceive the world and that the content of his experience is not subjective and relative: God experiences things just as they are in themselves, without bringing to bear any subjective contribution. But if so, then God does not perceive any secondary qualities; his perceptual experience represents things as we aspire to represent them in conception, i.e. from an absolute point of view. We might say that God's perceptual faculties constitute a perfection of those possessed by terrestrial beings. We may thus seem to have the notion of a form of ideal perception which requires pure unadulterated reflection of what is objectively present in the world.

Finally, an empiricist who wishes to make sense of an absolute and objective conception of things has a motive

---

[10] This sort of reason for expecting eliminability is likely to appeal to those who wish to explain perceptual content in terms of belief acquisition: e.g., G. Pitcher, *A Theory of Perception*—that is, if it is agreed that it is not necessary to have *beliefs* about secondary qualities.

for urging eliminability. Empiricists are apt to try to give content to concepts by envisaging what it would be to perceive their instantiation; and if a concept does not admit of such cashing out it is deemed suspect. In cases where our own perceptual faculties will not serve to underpin some problematic concept, it is tempting to postulate superior faculties of perception possessed by other beings which afford the requisite perceptual access to the world as thus conceived.[11] In line with this empiricist tendency, then, we will want to make sense of the possibility of a perceptual point of view embodying the objective conception we have ascribed to ourselves: perhaps *we* cannot perceive the world in the way we conceive it, but it is possible that *some* being should. Thus an empiricist will hold that the absolute conception is only contingently non-perceptual; and that *is* to hold that primary qualities can in principle be perceived without secondary qualities.

It should be noticed that none of these reasons for eliminating the subjective component from experience carries over to the objective component. We can equally ask whether secondary qualities can be perceived without primary qualities; but we do not find the same sorts of reasons for supposing that this ought to be possible. There is therefore nothing especially surprising about the contention that experience must be as of primary qualities; for if it were not, experience could not be *of* an objective world, since the objective world is precisely *constituted* by objects with primary qualities. For experience to reach out to the external spatial world at all it must represent the primary qualities of things. But this is precisely what we cannot say about the converse question, and so it becomes a real issue whether the eliminability of secondary quality experience is to be entertained. It seems to me, then, that there are a number of more or less respectable theoretical reasons for expecting secondary qualities to be eliminable from experience of the world, so that their

[11] Dummett gives explicit expression to this kind of idea (though in a rather different context): see his 'What is a Theory of Meaning? (II)', p. 99.

*in*eliminability would be philosophically significant and in need of some kind of explanation. But even if none of the above reasons is found at all compelling, we can still ask whether secondary qualities *are* in fact eliminable from experience, whether or not they *ought* to be, and what the ground of their ineliminability is, if they are ineliminable.

In *The Principles of Human Knowledge* Berkeley says: 'I desire any one to reflect whether he can, by any abstraction of thought, conceive the extension and motion of a body without all other sensible qualities. For my own part, I see evidently that it is not in my power to frame an idea of a body extended and moving, but I must withal give it some colour or other sensible quality which is acknowledged to exist in the mind. In short, extension, figure, and motion, abstracted from all other qualities, are inconceivable.'[12] And F. H. Bradley (among many others[13]) endorsed the point, writing: 'Extension cannot be presented, or thought of, except as one with quality that is secondary.'[14] Let us call this claim the *inseparability thesis*, and let us distinguish the application of the thesis to thought and to perception. Clearly, Berkeley and Bradley are, in insisting upon the inseparability thesis, denying the eliminability of the subjective aspect of perception (though they may not care to put it quite like that). And they are also committed to denying that we can make sense of an absolute and objective conception of things, given the subjectivity of secondary qualities. My own view is that we should reject this inseparability thesis for conception but accept it for perception. To take this divided attitude is to commit oneself to a radical

[12] Berkeley, *The Principles of Human Knowlege*, §10. Cf. *A New Theory of Vision*, XLIII and CXXII–CXXIII.

[13] For example, Husserl writes, of the alleged 'subtraction' of secondary qualities from primary qualities, that 'the old Berkeleian objection would hold good, namely, that extension, this essential nucleus of corporeality and all primary qualities, is unthinkable apart from the secondary qualities.' *Ideas*, §40. And Wittgenstein *seems* to have been saying something similar when he wrote: 'A speck in a visual field need not be red, but it must have a colour; it has, so to speak, a colour space round it. A tone must have *a* pitch, the object of the sense of touch *a* hardness, etc.' *Tractatus*, 2.0131.

[14] Bradley, *Appearance and Reality*, p. 14.

discontinuity between perception and conception: we cannot any longer regard conception as a kind of 'faint copy' of perception; it is not explicable in terms of an imagined perceptual point of view, indeed it is not strictly a point of *view* at all. So the temptation to try to picture or imagine the world as it is in itself, as God might perceive it, would be doomed to frustration and incoherence: it would then seem that the inseparability thesis about perception, combined with the availability of a purely objective conception of the world, lead to the conclusion that (certain kinds of) classical empiricist doctrines about concepts are fundamentally mistaken. In chapter 7 I shall say more on the relation between perception and the conception of things as they are in themselves; my present anticipatory point is that Berkeley's own position—that we cannot 'frame an idea' of body without ascribing secondary qualities to it—depends upon an imagist theory of concepts, and it is this that comes under pressure from the inseparability thesis about perception, if the objective conception is available.

In its full generality the inseparability thesis about perception says that for any actual and possible sense the content of experiences delivered by that sense must be both as of secondary qualities and as of primary qualities.[15] This means that no conceivable perceptual experience can fail to represent the world subjectively, as having qualities constituted by dispositions to produce experiences in the perceiver; and also (the converse) that the world must be perceived to have qualities which are not so subjectively constituted, viz. primary qualities.[16] Now it seems to me that both of these claims are

[15] The precise form of this claim is given by the following:

$\square \forall S$ (S gives experiences as of primary qualities iff S gives experiences as of secondary qualities),

where 'S' ranges over sense modalities; this says that all *possible* perceptual experience is as of *both* kinds of quality. This claim is to be distinguished from the thesis that a given sense necessarily gives the experiences of secondary qualities that it actually gives—for example, the thesis that vision necessarily involves the seeing of colour. This latter thesis is a claim about the essential properties of particular senses; it neither entails, nor is entailed by, the former claim about the conditions any possible sense must fulfil. I hold to both of these claims, but it is the former with which I am principally concerned in what follows.

[16] The Kantian thesis that all experience is (as) of objects in space has this as

true; in particular, Berkeley's claim seems to me to be a necessary truth about perception. Like Berkeley I take the inseparability thesis to be self-evident to reflection; and I do not know of any non-question-begging way to demonstrate its truth. However, I think the thesis cries out for some sort of explanation, which I will try to make progress towards below. But if it *is* true, then it is not trivially true; for it contradicts some initially attractive lines of thought about the possibilities of perception, e.g. the idea that God is a perceiver.

What does the inseparability thesis show about the objects of perception? Berkeley used the point to argue for idealism: 'if it be certain that these original [i.e. primary] qualities are inseparably united with other sensible [i.e. secondary] qualities, and not, even in thought, capable of being abstracted from them, it plainly follows that they exist only in the mind.'[17] This reasoning might be intended in either of two ways: as resting upon what it is possible to conceive, or as resting upon what forms of perception are possible. I have rejected the first claim and accepted the second; but it is worth seeing that Berkeley's argument fails under either interpretation. He relies upon a dubious principle and upon a tendentious characterisation of what it is for a quality to be secondary. The dubious principle is to the effect that if a quality Q is subjectively constituted, and if a quality P cannot be conceived as instantiated except in items in which Q also is, then P must itself be subjectively constituted. On reflection this seems a palpable *non sequitur*: why should subjectivity be transmitted through necessary co-instantiation? Suppose aesthetic properties to be subjective, and suppose

a consequence, since spatial properties are the paradigm of primary qualities. Even smell and taste fall under this thesis because they necessarily represent their objects as in some spatial relation to the perceiver's body (e.g. in his mouth). (There is a good discussion of this in some forthcoming work of Michael Ayers on perception, to which I am indebted at this point.)

[17] Berkeley, *Principles*, § 10. In *A New Theory of Vision*, XLIII, Berkeley gives essentially the same argument, except that he there relies upon the idea that the perceived *location* of primary qualities is the same as that of secondary qualities—and these latter he takes to be within (spatially!) the mind.

that every conceivable object must be conceived to have
some aesthetic property—beautiful, ugly, neutral; it obviously
would not follow that *all* other properties of objects are
themselves subjective. This principle recommends itself to
Berkeley because he has a special interpretation of what it is
for a quality to be subjective, which is not Locke's: Berkeley
takes it that secondary qualities are 'in the mind' in the sense
that they are to be *predicated* of the experiences themselves,
and not of the external objects which have certain dispositions in respect of experience. He then feels able to invoke
the principle that primary and secondary qualities are instantiated by the same items, thus making the former into
attributes of experiences also. But this idealist argument can
be resisted simply by insisting upon the weaker Lockean
interpretation of 'in the mind', and then rejecting Berkeley's
principle about co-instantiation.

Berkeley was clearly directing his point against Locke,
apparently committing Locke to holding that there can be
perception without the ascription of secondary qualities:
for Locke held (correctly I think) that things in themselves
have only primary qualities and that we can conceive of them
as they are in themselves.[18] And given Locke's broadly
empiricist view about concepts, we might expect him to
embrace the perceptual separability of primary from secondary qualities. There is indeed a passage in Locke which is
naturally taken to express just this possibility, headed 'The
Now Secondary Qualities of Bodies would disappear, if we
could discover the primary ones of their Minute Parts', which
is worth extended quotation:

Had we senses acute enough to discern the minute particles of bodies,
and the real constitution on which their sensible qualities depend, I
doubt not but they would produce quite different ideas in us; and that

---

[18] As exegesis of Locke this needs a qualification, because Locke is generally
unwilling to suppose that we cognitively limited creatures can really form an
objective conception of the world: but he does appear to think that this is a
logically possible conception—it is the kind possessed by God. I should thus
more cautiously say that Locke's view is that we know that such a conception
exists, though we cannot realistically hope to attain it.

which is now the yellow colour of gold would then disappear, and instead of it we should see an admirable texture of parts, of a certain size and figure. This microscopes plainly discover to us; for what to our naked eyes produces a certain colour, is, by thus augmenting the acuteness of our senses, discovered to be quite a different thing; and thus altering, as it were, the proportion of the bulk of the minute parts of a coloured object to our usual sight produces different ideas from what it did before. Thus, sand or pounded glass, which is opaque, and white to the naked eye, is pellucid in a microscope; and a hair seen in this way loses its former colour, and is, in great measure, pellucid, with a mixture of some bright sparkling colours, such as appear from the refraction of diamonds, and other pellucid bodies. Blood, to the naked eye, appears all red; but by a good microscope, wherein its lesser parts appear, shows only some few globules of red, swimming in a pellucid liquor, and how these globules would appear, if glasses could be found that yet could magnify them a thousand or ten thousand times more, is uncertain.[19]

What is chiefly interesting about this passage is the ambivalence, not to say vacillation, that it displays over whether 'microscopical eyes' would reveal colour in normally imperceptible things. Locke begins by suggesting, or seeming to suggest, that *only* primary qualities would be seen by such eyes, but then goes on to say in effect that *different* secondary qualities would be revealed to acuter senses than ours, though he tries (vainly) to recover the spirit of his initial suggestion by saying that things look 'pellucid' under microscopes. It is thus very difficult to decide which thesis Locke is putting forward in this passage; my suspicion is that he felt obliged by his empiricist theory of concepts to give perceptual content to the conception we have of things in themselves, but then he hesitated to do so because of the force of the inseparability thesis which he subliminally acknowledged. In this passage we see Locke confronting the problem of how an empiricist can allow for an absolute conception of things, once he accepts Berkeley's inseparability claim (not *explicitly* of course). But it is, at any rate, unclear that Locke ever really endorsed the claim about perception against which Berkeley's point is directed—which shows Locke's good judgement, if not his theoretical penetration.

More recent philosophers have, however, explicitly accepted

---

[19] Locke, *Essay*, II, xxiii, 11.

the claim about the possibilities of perception which Locke very properly hesitated to affirm, and they have done so as part of a defence of the Lockean conception of physical objects. That is to say, they take it that the Lockean conception can only be maintained if the Berkeley point is denied; whereas I want to preserve the Lockean conception by holding that it is not a perceptual style of mental representation at all. I thus incur the obligation to explain the nature of the absolute conception, but I avoid the implausibility of denying the inseparability thesis. Recent philosophers have tried to reduce the implausibility I avoid in a number of ways. Bennett agrees that the Berkeley point is compelling for vision, but says (or seems to say) that touch provides experience of primary qualities without experience of any secondary qualities.[20] This strikes me as simply false; for surely the content of tactile experiences includes felt temperature and this is a dispositional sensory quality.[21] Armstrong tells us that we experience no colour when we see things 'out of the corner of our eye';[22] but this is dubious in itself and hardly enough to justify the notion of a total visual field in which no colours (including achromatic colours) are experienced. Campbell distinguishes between seeing colour *differences* and seeing colour *qualities*, and he suggests that while the

[20] Bennett, *Locke, Berkeley, Hume*, pp. 90–4.

[21] It might be retorted that, though temperature is in fact always associated in tactile experience with shape, size, etc., this is just a contingent fact—we can imagine a kind of tactile experience which lacks this type of content but is otherwise phenomenologically indistinguishable from our actual tactile experience. However, I think this is not as clearly possible as one might be tempted to imagine, especially if we are careful to exclude *all* degrees of temperature. But even if it were possible, there would be other felt qualities in tactile experience which would not be objective properties of the objects of touch—I mean those relating to hardness and softness, pressure, etc. The associated types of sensation are specific to touch, and we can characterise objects in terms of their dispositions to produce such sensations, thus recording the presence of tactile secondary qualities.

[22] Armstrong, 'Perception, Sense Data and Causality', p. 84. He asks us to accept that 'Our perceptions themselves act as permanent coloured spectacles' (loc. cit.)—which, presumably, we manage to see round when something appears on the far periphery of the visual field. I suspect Armstrong is here misled by the fact that we do not always *notice* (in one sense) the colour of what is visually perceived.

former is necessary to visual perception the latter is not, thus undercutting (as he thinks) the Berkeley point.[23] But it seems to me just unintelligible to suppose that one could register differences of colour and not register the colours them-selves—what would it be *like* to have such a visual field? Jackson says that panes of glass are perceptible objects yet they possess rather few secondary qualities, and he invites us to imagine a kind of physical object from which *all* secon-dary qualities have been stripped and which is perceivable as such.[24] But surely this is inconceivable: Jackson must hold that an object of this etiolated kind could be seen, but I cannot imagine what it would be to see something with size and shape and no colour. I can of course imagine what it would be to look at something transparent, but then my visual field contains the colours of things lying behind the transparent object—I do not, however, know what the world would look like if *all* objects of vision were totally transparent. None of these suggestions would, I think, exercise any attraction were it not for the theoretical motives which seem to require them: but I suggest that we abandon the theory of concepts which requires the objective conception to consti-tute a possible form of perception rather than burden our-selves with these counterintuitive claims.

A more challenging line of objection to the inseparability thesis about perception arises from the thought that elemen-tary particles are colourless.[25] The proposition that elementary particles are colourless is supposed to follow from the facts

[23] Campbell, 'Colours', pp. 148–9. He concludes: 'There is a real sense in which perception of colour is a needless luxury even in the *visual* perception of shape; the Berkeleian objection pitches too high the dependence of perception of shape on the perception of colour'; for (Campbell claims) we can become visually aware of shape just by detecting a colour *boundary*—we do not need to experi-ence the specific colours that define the boundary. Again, I think this can seem plausible only if we illicitly restrict experiential content to what is noticed— in the sense of that which one is able to report in the content of a visual glimpse.

[24] Jackson, *Perception*, p. 130. He does not distinguish between the insepar-ability thesis with respect to how things can be in themselves and with respect to how they can be perceptually represented.

[25] Armstrong alludes to this question, though in a somewhat different con-nexion: see *A Materialist Theory of the Mind*, pp. 282–3.

about their physical properties: they cannot have the absorp-
tion and reflection properties in respect of light which constitute the ground of the power to cause colour experience
in perceivers. If we conjoin the claim that particles are
colourless with the inseparability thesis, we get the result that
the minute constituents of matter are logically unperceivable
—which is embarrassing, if not absurd. For surely electrons
are only contingently invisible, despite their lack of colour?
I think that the right reply to this argument is to distinguish
two senses of 'colourless': to say an electron is colourless might
mean that it cannot as things are produce colour experience,
i.e. cannot interact with light in the requisite way; or it might
mean that it (the electron) could not in any possible circumstances look to have a certain colour, i.e. could not have the
power to produce colour experience *by any mechanism*. In
the former sense we can say, plausibly, that electrons are
colourless and necessarily so, since they could not, compatibly
with the laws of physics, interact with light in the way that
normally produces colour experience; but it does not follow
that they are colourless in the second sense, since they might
be capable of producing colour experience in perceivers in
some different way, e.g. by way of their electric charge and
some suitably sensitive sensory receptors.[26] I think that
electrons may be said to have colour (at least potentially) in
the second sense, but not in the first: so *if* we could see them
they *would* have colour, but not by virtue of the usual
physical mechanism. In other words, electrons could *look*
coloured otherwise than by means of the reflection of light;
but then, by the dispositional analysis of colour, they would
be coloured. So electrons are only contingently colourless,
despite the fact that necessarily they cannot interact with

[26] We could put the point in terms of a scope ambiguity in 'electrons necessarily lack the basis of the power to produce colour experiences': if we read this
as 'concerning the (actual) basis of the power to produce colour experiences,
electrons necessarily lack it', then the claim is (I think) true; but it does not
follow, and is not true, that 'necessarily: electrons lack the basis of the power to
produce colour experience', since the phrase 'the basis of the power' could stand
for a different basis from the actual basis and that different basis be (possibly)
possessed by electrons.

light in the way that normally produces colour experience. The only way to move from the first idea of colourlessness to the second—i.e. from lack of the normal physical basis to the necessary lack of colour as a dispositional property—is to presuppose a reductionist view of colour. It is indeed true that on a reductionist view electrons are necessarily colourless; but *we* need not be embarrassed by this consequence, because we reject the reductionist view. I think, in fact, that the inseparability thesis plus the merely contingent imperceptibility of elementary particles together constitute strong argument against a reductionist position on colours.[27]

It seems to me, then, that the Berkeley point stands. But what does it show? I think it shows nothing about how things are in themselves: specifically, it does not show that objects are after all objectively coloured and so intrinsically demand to be so represented. That it does not show this is evident from the inapplicability of the point to conception: for we *can* conceive objects purely in terms of primary qualities; so the inseparability thesis about perception has no tendency to annihilate the difference, in point of objectivity, between primary and secondary qualities. What is shown is rather how *perceptual consciousness* necessarily is: it is a necessary truth about experience itself that it represent things as having secondary qualities. Berkeley took the point to show something about the essential nature of the objects of experience; I take it to show something about the essential nature of the experience of objects. To put it in the terms made familiar in chapter 3, the inseparability thesis is a law of subjectivity: it tells us how things can perceptually *seem*. This way of understanding the matter liberates us from the fear that the

---

[27] I might insert a remark here about the alleged problem of how individually colourless particles could compose a coloured macroscopic object. The obvious answer is that the power to produce colour experience is only possessed by particles in *aggregates*: as things are, they lack this power taken singly, but that does not prevent them composing larger objects which do have the power as a result of properties of their constitutive particles. This seems to me no more difficult to understand than the 'problem' of how a lump of sugar can be soluble given that it is made up of elements which are not themselves soluble: it is just that this disposition is possessed only by aggregates of such elements.

Lockean conception of objects is somehow contra-indicated by the necessary features of experience, because those features have their source in subjective experience itself and not in the objective world of which we have experience. There are thus two sorts of reason why features of our mental representations may present themselves as indispensable: either because the feature belongs to the world as it is in itself and so demands to be recognised; or because the faculty of representation in question itself imposes the feature on the represented world, i.e. the ineliminability arises from a law of subjectivity. My suggestion is that the perception of secondary qualities is an instance of the second type: we might say that it is a *de re* necessity of conscious perceptual experience.[28] This interpretation of the necessity in question also enables us to resist the suggestion that the objects of conception and perception are distinct objects; for it is not that the represented *objects* differ in their intrinsic nature— it is rather that the means of *representing* them do.[29] So I place the Berkeley point along with the other *a priori* necessities of experience I discussed in chapter 3; and the same kinds of reasons for regarding those as irreducible apply also in the present case. Thus, for example, it could not be maintained that the necessity for an object with extension to have colour reduces to the necessity for extended objects to reflect light of certain wavelengths; for this lacks the epistemic and modal features attaching to the original proposition about colour itself. Moreover, as we just saw, the inseparability thesis applies also at the level of elementary

---

[28] I say 'conscious' because so-called 'unconscious perception' might be thought not to involve, of necessity, the perception of secondary qualities: this kind of 'perception' consists in a pre-experiential sensitivity to primary qualities which need not be accompanied by sensitivity to secondary qualities. I do not wish to deny that we may use the word 'perception' to describe such phenomena, though I would jib at supposing there to be anything of the nature of genuine *experience* involved; my claim is then limited to conscious experiential awareness. In fact, I think that the holding of the inseparability thesis can be seen as a criterion for something's being an instance of genuine conscious perceptual experience.

[29] Husserl seems to infer the ontological distinctness of the objects of perception and the objects of science from the Berkeley point: see *Ideas*, p. 128.

particles, but for them the objectivist reduction is unworkable: the proper interpretation of the Berkeley point is rather that nothing could *look* to have a particular shape (etc.) without also *looking* to have a particular colour. The reciprocal dependence of primary and secondary qualities which is manifest in experience is precisely a dependence in the realm of how things can seem.[30] This makes it intelligible why conception does not likewise conform to the inseparability thesis: it is because conception does not have the phenomenological character which defines the field of application of the laws of subjectivity; the discontinuity we detected between the two styles of mental representation is thus bound up with the differential applicability of the laws of subjectivity. Thought is not constrained by the same principles that determine the possibilities of perception. And thought is what represents how things are objectively, not perception.[31]

I can perhaps bring out the structure of the issue by considering some parallels with indexicals. Suppose it is claimed that we cannot conceive of space and time and selves without locating these items in an indexical perspective, without representing them under indexical concepts. Then, in view of the subjective or egocentric character of indexical representation, it would follow that we are constrained to think of the world in a centred subject-involving way. This is a thesis of the ineliminability of the subjective view, as exemplified by indexical thought. How should we react to it? We should first distinguish two questions: does the ineliminability thesis apply to all species of thought? and does it apply to the kind of thought which is based upon direct

[30] Indeed, this law of subjectivity does not imply a corresponding necessity of being: for we cannot properly say 'nothing could *have* primary qualities without also *having* secondary qualities', since (in a certain sense) objects would *not* have secondary qualities if there were no perceivers to perceive them. The necessity in question is thus *purely* phenomenological.

[31] So we cannot suppose that a theory of intentional content for belief and for experience will be unitary: in particular, we cannot hope to explain the representational content of experience as just a special case of belief content, as belief acquisition theories of perception try to do. Propensities to form beliefs are more 'atomistic' than the content of experience; they can be possessed independently in a way that aspects of experiential content cannot.

cognitive awareness of the world? For it seems that there is a distinction to be drawn, analogous to that drawn between conception and perception in respect of secondary qualities, between thought which is free of contamination by the subjective viewpoint (i.e. non-indexical thought) and thought which exploits the subjective viewpoint by using the self as an anchor point (i.e. indexical thought). Thus physics and mathematics and other sciences do not employ indexical propositions: the world is conceptualized without selecting any particular point of view as privileged. And for this kind of thought the ineliminability thesis about indexicals strikes us as wrong—as it was for secondary qualities. But there is also the kind of thought we operate with when actively engaged in the world, when the world is directly presented to our consciousness; and this seems shot through with indexicality. Here the ineliminability thesis looks much more plausible: for it is indeed hard to make sense of such direct cognitive awareness without the presence of indexical modes of presentation. What would it be to have direct acquaintance with oneself and yet not think of oneself as 'I', and how could it be possible to be presented with the present time (at that time) and not think of it as 'now'?[32] It thus seems that what the phenomenologists would call 'being-in-the-world' presupposes indexical thought. Let us, if only for the sake of argument, go along with the ineliminability thesis so stated; we can then foresee three possible reactions to the thesis. Some might wish to infer that space and time and selves have a subjective intrinsic nature: since we cannot separate our thought about them from involvement with our own subjective perspective, this must show

[32] Similarly, perceptual judgements necessarily involve demonstrative concepts. In all these cases to be acquainted with an item in the world requires that it be brought under a concept whose content relates to the subject of acquaintance, i.e. an egocentric concept: thus the relation of acquaintance between subject and object is necessarily mediated by concepts whose application conditions make essential reference to that very subject. Similarly, to have perceptual experience of an object the object must be perceived to have qualities whose instantiation conditions make essential reference to properties of the perceiver, i.e. to the kinds of experience he enjoys.

that it is in their very nature to be subjective—they are really aspects of our subjective make-up. This response, however, is somewhat compromised by restricting the inelimin-ability thesis to direct awareness; the existence of another non-indexical mode of conception shows that our representa-tions of the world *can* be innocent of subjective elements.[33] Acknowledging this difference, a second reaction is to insist upon distinguishing, numerically, the *objects* of the two styles of representation: there is the space and time of physics, but there is also the space and time of direct con-scious awareness; and the former is objective in nature while the latter is constitutionally subjective.[34] The third response, which I favour, is to interpret the ineliminability thesis, not as indicative of how space and time are in themselves, but rather as showing something about us and our faculties of representation: that is, the thesis states a necessary truth about what it is to have direct cognitive awareness of space and time. Just as there is one world onto which both percep-tion and conception may be directed, despite the different role of secondary qualities in the two sorts of representation, so there is one world onto which indexical and non-indexical thought are directed, despite the essential differences between these styles of thought. This simple truth about the objects of mental representation, e.g. space and time, is held in place by interpreting the ineliminability of indexical concepts as a law of subjectivity, not as revelatory of the objective or intrinsic nature of what is thought about. To move from the ineliminability thesis to an idealist or subjectivist conception of space and time as they are in themselves, on analogy with Berkeley's idealist argument about perceptible objects, begins to look no more warranted than inferring the intrinsic

---

[33] It does not yet follow that this other mode of representation better reveals the true nature of reality; it merely shows that we are not *forced* to represent reality subjectively, and so have the means to show how a rejection of idealism can be squared with the possibilities of thought: the nature of mental representa-tion does not then make idealism *mandatory*.

[34] Such a view was held by Russell: see, e.g. *Human Knowledge: Its Scope and Limits*, pp. 280 ff., and 'Sense Data and Physics'.

subjectivity of length from the fact that equal lines must look unequal in the Muller–Lyer illusion. The basic point here is just that our *faculties* may be such as to make it necessary that things be represented as having certain properties without it following that those properties are possessed by things objectively or intrinsically. When we learn that a certain kind of item must appear to us (or to any being) in a certain way there are thus always two possible explanations of this: either it is because that is the way the item objectively and intrinsically is; or it is because the mode of apprehension through which it appears is itself responsible for its having to appear that way. My claim has been that objects must appear to have primary qualities for the first sort of reason, but they must appear to have secondary qualities for the second sort of reason. Somewhat similarly, the indexical properties of space and time which we ineluctably ascribe in direct cognitive awareness have their source in our faculties, whereas the non-indexical properties of space and time (e.g. their metrical properties) are ascribed in acknowledgement of their objective intrinsic nature. (This is why it is tempting—though a bit incautious—to say that before there were perceivers there were no secondary qualities, and that before there were thinkers there were no indexical properties: it is a dramatic way of registering the fact that the ascription of these features to the world must always go through reference to a subject of awareness from which they spring.) The question of the significance of ineliminability correspondingly takes on a new aspect once this distinction is accepted. A feature can (to repeat) be ineliminable from our representations either because we aim to cover all that is objectively present in the world and the feature in question has this status, or it can be ineliminable because to eliminate it would be to be deprived of a certain kind of mental faculty. When we try to envisage a being devoid of indexical concepts and perception of secondary qualities his lack does not consist in failing to register an objective feature of the world, a feature the world has independently of conscious beings; his lack consists rather in being deprived of the faculties of perception and direct awareness, since what he is stipulated to be devoid of is constitutive of having those faculties. Ineliminability from our mental representations thus has a quite different significance according as it has one or the other explanation; and the cardinal error of (some) idealistically inclined philosophers has been to interpret ineliminability as having significance with respect to how things are in themselves instead of with respect to our epistemic faculties.

So much for the metaphysical significance of the ineliminability theses; we must now enquire into their explanation or ground. Granted what I have said about their significance, the direction in which their explanation is to be sought is already determined: if they are explicable at all, it will be in virtue of some feature of our mental faculties. Thus, in particular, it will be some necessary feature of perceptual experience which explains why it must always be as of secondary qualities, some requirement experience imposes upon its content which perception of secondary qualities fulfils.[35] Now I am not at all sure that any such explanation can ultimately be given; it may be that the necessity in question is brute and primitive, a fundamental datum about perceptual experience. But I think that the reasons I set out which seemed to favour eliminability do at least make it reasonable to look for an explanation; one feels that it *ought* to be somehow intelligible that experience necessarily has subjective content as well as objective content. In an effort to provide some sort of

---

[35] I should make it quite clear that what I am seeking an explanation for is the claim that any possible sense must give experiences as of secondary qualities; I am not concerned in what follows with *de re* necessities in respect of the secondary qualities actual senses afford perception of, e.g. the necessity that vision give experiences of colour. While I do not think these latter necessities are in any way trivial, they do not seem to me to call for explanation in the way the generalised inseparability thesis does: they require as much explanation (or as little) as other more familiar kinds of *de re* necessities, e.g. that water is necessarily H_2O or that Caesar is necessarily a man. For these are (synthetic) truths about what properties make something the thing it is, rather than (as the inseparability thesis is) conditions on what can count as perceptual experience quite generally: these particular *de re* necessities are thus not as philosophically surprising as the generalised inseparability thesis is.

rationale of the Berkeley point, as I have interpreted it, I shall therefore consider three possible theories of the matter; the first two I shall reject, the third I shall tentatively put forward as at least worth thinking about.

(i) *The medium theory.* This theory of secondary quality experience has been explicitly advocated by C. Hooker, though hints of it are discernible in other authors; I am adapting it to my own purposes in what follows.[36] In a nutshell, the theory is that perception of secondary qualities constitutes the medium through which primary qualities are perceived: 'We distinguish sharply between the information encoded and the mode or medium of its encoding. The information is the origin of the objective component of visual experience, the mode and medium provide the origin of the subjective component of the experience. (Being aware of colour is intimately bound up with being aware of the character of the encoding medium.) Both components are consciously experienced together as the *embedding* of one in the other: we perceive coloured shape.'[37] The idea is that when an object is perceived two elements in the content of the experience must be distinguished: awareness of the primary quality information supplied by the object, and awareness of the conscious medium in which this information is presented, this latter being experience of the object's secondary qualities. Secondary quality experience, we might say, functions as the *material* from which perceptual representations of primary qualities are made; its role is analogous to that of syntax (or phonology) in relation to semantic properties. A semantic informational content is represented in a syntactic object (a sentence) as its medium; Hooker's suggestion is that when we perceive an object we have two kinds of awareness, syntactic and semantic in character, corresponding to the subjective and objective contents of

[36] Clifford Hooker, 'An Evolutionary Naturalist Realist Doctrine of Perception and Secondary Qualities'. I think Hooker makes very explicit what is often inchoately supposed.

[37] Hooker, op. cit., p. 424.

the experience respectively. This is an arresting theory, and it has the great merit of recognising that some explanation is called for as to why secondary qualities are perceived at all in view of their subjective nature. Its application to the inseparability thesis should be obvious enough: the reason primary qualities cannot be perceived without perceiving secondary qualities is just that all information must be encoded in some medium, and the medium in the case of perceptual consciousness is awareness of colour, taste, etc.[38] Do not ask *why* this is the medium of perceptual representation of primary qualities and not some other property; it is the medium because that is what (on this theory) conscious experience *is*, just as spatial arrangements of marks on paper constitute the medium of written meaning. We can mentally represent primary qualities otherwise than perceptually, but if conscious perceptual experience is the means of representation then it will bring to bear its own distinctive materials of representation.[39] On this view, then, Berkeley's point has roughly this force: perception without secondary qualities would be like a message without a medium; it is like trying to express a proposition without using any words. It would be as if we wanted to employ a specific form of representation but refused to countenance its distinctive medium. The medium theory has, I think, the *form* of an explanation of the inseparability thesis: it deduces that thesis from certain general considerations, of the required modal status, about the nature of representation: but

[38] Hooker does not exploit the medium theory to explain the Berkeley point; indeed he disavows adherence to that point (see note 19, op. cit. p. 347). He even goes so far as to deny that colour is the necessary medium of *visual* perception, apparently envisaging the possibility of a kind of vision whose medium consisted in some quite different kind of phenomenal (?) quality. His position would thus appear to be that, while perception of secondary qualities is the *actual* medium of sensory awareness of primary qualities, other sorts of medium are in principle conceivable. Needless to say, I disagree.

[39] In other words, every means of representation has some intrinsic nature, and this nature will give rise to necessities in the properties of the representing medium: it is in the nature of perceptual consciousness (on this theory) to represent the world through the medium of secondary qualities, since these *constitute* its nature *qua* mode of representation.

unfortunately it suffers from a number of serious defects. The main defect, of course, is that the medium theory is committed to a very radical error theory of sensory experience: phenomenologically, secondary qualities are perceived as properties of the same items to which primary qualities are ascribable, but on the medium theory that is, literally, an illusion. Subjection to this illusion must seem a great puzzle to the medium theory, for we do not typically confuse medium and message in this ineradicable way: it is as if someone were compelled to believe that Smith has five letters because his name does, or that Jones is red because his name is written in red ink. According to the medium theory, experience itself is inherently confused about use and mention, irresistibly transferring properties of the symbol onto that which it symbolises; the error is thus yet more egregious than under other sorts of error theory. Hooker himself does not flinch from this consequence of the medium theory, declaring that our senses commit an error of 'objectification' which puts us under a 'systematic illusion'.[40] It is bad enough to be committed to this consequence, but matters are made worse by the unavailability of any sort of explanation of *why* our senses necessarily subject us to this illusion.[41] Secondly, it appears implausible to restrict the information-bearing aspect of experience to its primary quality content: surely we learn something about an *object* when we discover its secondary qualities, in a way we learn nothing of a man when we discover how many letters his name has. If secondary quality experience were informationally inert, its variety would be something of a puzzle: why not employ the *same* medium for all primary quality information—as we might employ the same colour ink for all written documents? Moreover, it is plainly untrue

---

[40] Hooker, op. cit., pp. 424 ff.

[41] Why should experience of secondary qualities be representational at all on the medium theory? If secondary qualities are really properties of the medium, why do they not present themselves as *intrinsic* properties of experience, i.e. as non-representational features on a par with (e.g.) the duration of an experience or its place of occurrence? Hooker has no satisfactory explanation of this.

that secondary qualities tell us nothing about objects save the character of the medium in which we represent them: colour (as every bee knows) contains information about which plants to alight on, and taste obviously contains information about things. On the medium theory, such information would be as worthless as the 'information' that Jones is red derived from the colour of (a token of) his name. For these reasons (among others[42]) I do not think the medium theory provides a satisfactory explanation of the inseparability thesis.

(ii) *The utility theory*. This theory takes seriously the idea that secondary qualities contain information, that the perception of them has a function. Primary quality perception gives information about the objective world; secondary quality perception, according to the utility theory, gives information about the relation between the perceptual object and the perceiver's needs and interests. This type of theory is put forward by both Descartes and Locke to explain the role of secondary qualities, granted their subjectivist accounts of them.[43] Again, I applaud their seeing the desirability of an explanation once the subjectivist account is accepted. Descartes' view is (roughly) that men have an intellectual faculty which employs only primary quality concepts—this faculty provides properly theoretical knowledge of the world; but we have also been endowed by God with faculties fitting us to 'the conduct of life', and these enable us to detect the secondary qualities of things which are so closely connected with what is beneficial and harmful to us. To put it in

---

[42] One further problem is that the medium theory gives no guarantee that the features of experience which constitute the medium of its representational content should be secondary qualities in the classical sense: that is, we have no explanation of the *dispositionality* of the qualities that comprise the medium. It is not enough to reply that this is just a primitive inexplicable fact about perceptual consciousness: for the question is why *this* medium should give rise to *such* qualities when the media of other systems of representation do not. Any satisfying explanation of the Berkeley point should show the significance of the dispositional–relational character of secondary qualities.

[43] See Descartes, *Meditations*, VI; Locke, *Essay*, II, xxii, 12. I am not suggesting that Descartes and Locke conceived their theory in precisely the way I do here.

post-Darwinian terms, evolution has equipped us (and other animals) with the ability to perceive secondary qualities because these put us on to properties of things which are crucial to survival. We could say that secondary qualities afford interest-relative classifications of things; they classify in a way which is determined by the organism's needs. Purely theoretical knowledge prescinds from our needs and interests, and so it can ignore secondary qualites; but practical knowledge of the world requires that it be represented in an interest-relative way—and the perception of secondary qualities fulfils this function. According to the utility theory, then, the inseparability thesis is true because perceptual experience without experience of secondary qualities would not have the practical role it must have if the perceiving organism is to use its perceptual faculties to aid survival. Now I do not wish to disagree with what the utility theory says about the biological role of secondary quality perception, nor with the Cartesian distinction between practical and theoretical faculties and the relation of this distinction to the distinction between primary and secondary qualites. But I do not think that the utility theory can really explain the Berkeleian inseparability thesis.[44] The problem is that the inseparability thesis is a *necessary* truth about experience, but it appears only *contingent* that a creature's perceptual experiences have a biological function. It is not enough to explain why we evolved creatures do *in fact* perceive secondary qualities; we have also to explain why any conceivable perceiving creature *must*. Construed as a would-be explanation of this modal fact, the utility theory would have the consequence that perceptual experience is necessarily useful to survival; and this seems implausible. The problem is that the necessity to be explained arises from the very nature of experience itself; it does not present itself as a more or less adventitious consequence of the fact that perceivers (actually) have needs and interests. Perhaps the utility theory can explain why a

---

[44] I do not say that Descartes and Locke undertook to explain the inseparability thesis; they did not, so far as I know, acknowledge any such thesis.

creature perceives these rather than those secondary qualities, but it does not have the power to explain why, as a matter of necessity, any are perceived at all. Furthermore, it is unclear that utility considerations are *sufficient* to explain why secondary qualities are perceived (we have just seen that they are not necessary): for why should the interest-relative properties of things not be represented in primary quality terms? It will not do to answer that this would be much less efficient from an evolutionary point of view—that, for example, it is much more convenient to decide whether something is nourishing on the basis of how it tastes rather than by knowing its chemical analysis and one's own digestive requirements. This is certainly true, but again it does not constitute an in-principle obstacle to perception without secondary qualities: microscopic eyes and extensive knowledge of physiology could perform the same function as tasting does, but secondary qualities would still have to be perceived.[45] If the interest-relative information carried by secondary qualities can be carried in some other way, then we would expect the utility theory to allow that logically possible perceivers could dispense with secondary quality experience; but we know that this is impossible. These objections to the utility theory as an account of the inseparability thesis are not, to repeat, intended to cut against what Descartes and Locke say about the *de facto* function of perceiving secondary qualities; what they refute is rather the attempt to explain Berkeley's modal point in terms of their theory.

---

[45] Thus a scientist can classify things as edible or inedible on behalf of an animal with different digestive requirement from his own, so this information can be represented by other means than taste: the question is then why there could not be a sense whose experiential content contained this information directly, instead of by means of the secondary qualities of taste. Or again, boundaries of objects can be detected otherwise than by way of colour, so why should there not be a kind of vision whose content contains information about boundaries in this other way? It does not seem that any interest-relative classification can be effected *only* by means of perceived secondary qualities, and so this means would seem in principle dispensable.

(iii) *The intentionality theory.* We can come at this theory by first considering the converse inseparability thesis—namely, that it is impossible to perceive secondary qualities without perceiving primary qualities. The natural explanation of this necessity is that perceptual experience is necessarily as of an external world of spatially disposed objects, and these objects are objectively characterised by primary qualities: experience could not be of what is objective and spatial unless it represented its objects as having primary qualities. It is constitutive of objects in space to have determinate primary qualities; so it is constitutive of experience being *as of* such objects that it have primary quality content. This explains the necessity in question because it is derived from a general and essential feature of perceptual experience, viz. its outer-directedness.[46] But of course this explanation just accentuates the question why secondary qualities must be perceived, because this is precisely what we *cannot* say about perception of them—secondary qualities are not constitutive of the idea of an external and objective world. Indeed, it is the naturalness of the picture of perception employed by the explanation of the converse inseparability thesis—to wit, that perception reflects the objective world—that makes it seem a pressing question why secondary qualities are perceived at all. Experience has an objective component because its business is to represent an objective world; but this cannot be why it also has a subjective content. If we tried to adapt that sort of explanation to the latter case, we would get the result

[46] This is really a composite thesis: first, that things are necessarily perceived as disposed in space; second, that things perceived as disposed in space must be perceived to have primary qualities. The first part of this composite thesis might be taken as primitive, or one might hope to derive it from the more basic truth that objects of perception must be *independent* of being perceived and space uniquely provides for such independence. The second part is a consequence of the first because the notion of the occupancy of space requires the possession of primary (especially geometrical) qualities. It is worth noting that the objects of perception must also be (perceived as) temporal, i.e. that they are essentially related to events standing in temporal relations (unlike numbers, say); and temporal relations are themselves primary qualities. If perceptual experience did not represent its objects in terms of these primary qualities, it could not be said to represent anything 'outer' at all, and so could not qualify as perceptual.

that perception, in so far as it is of secondary qualities, is designed to represent the subjective constitution of the perceiver! Aside from being unintelligible, this explanation would make the perception of secondary qualities seem like a deficiency, something that hinders the proper purpose of perceiving. We need an explanation that demonstrates how the *outer*-directedness of perception is contributed to by perceiving secondary qualities, despite their subjectivity.

The intentionality theory accordingly claims that it is precisely *because of* their subjectivity that secondary qualities contribute to the outer-directedness of perception. The form of the theory is this: perception is necessarily of primary qualitied objects; but its being so is in a certain way *dependent* upon perception of secondary qualities; hence there cannot be the former without the latter. The question is exactly in what way the dependence works. Intuitively, the idea is that while perception of primary qualities makes for experience of *objects*, perception of secondary qualities makes for *experience of* objects—it is the mechanism of perceptual intentionality. We might say, metaphorically, that secondary qualities establish a sort of bridge between the perceiving subject and the external object; they serve to bring objects into direct contact with the mind. They do this by way of their relationality or subject-involvingness: primary qualitied objects engage with conscious experience by interacting with the perceiver's subjective constitution, i.e. the specific sensory receptivities which determine which secondary qualities will be perceived. Secondary qualities thus operate to establish an 'internal' relation between mind and object, a relation in which both the antecedent constitution of the mind and that of the world are brought together. If, *per impossibile*, perception were just of primary qualities, there would not be this engagement with an antecedent subjective constitution; the mind would merely mirror the world in an 'external' way. Secondary qualities can function as the mechanism of perceptual intentionality because they face in two directions: they are genuine properties of the external object, and they are also defined by the experience they produce. The first characteristic enables perception of them to reach out to objective things; the second is what makes it the case that a mind with an intrinsic nature is what reaches out. This reconciles two aspects of secondary qualities which have seemed to many to be in tension: that they are perceived as, and indeed are, properties of external objects; and that they are nevertheless subjectively constituted. The intentionality theory claims that this is precisely what we should expect, given their role—to act as a bridge between subject and object. To the old question 'how does the mind get into immediate contact with external things?' the intentionality theory has the answer 'by perceiving them as having secondary qualities'. This theory (or sketch of a theory) explains the inseparability thesis by saying that experience of seconday qualities is necessary because without it perceptual intentionality would be impossible: denying the inseparability thesis thus amounts to wanting perception to take place without its essential mechanism. Perception results from the coming together of a prior mental constitution and an objectively determined world; secondary qualities are what cross the interface. The subjective component of perceptual content establishes an internal relation between outer and inner; the objective component cannot do this on its own, because it relates wholly to what is outer.

I would be the first to admit that the intentionality theory is obscure and outlandish, but I think it is worth pondering (a) because it does seem to have some intuitive force as a theory of perception, and (b) because it promises to explain the Berkeley point, which seems desirable.[47] So far as I can see, the choice is between accepting the intentionality theory and conceding that the inseparability thesis is primitive and inexplicable. Taking the latter alternative is not altogether easy to live with; but it *may* be that the urge to explain the

[47] And also because it can be philosophically illuminating to see to what lengths one may be forced to go in giving an account of something that needs to be made intelligible—it heightens one's sense of the problem. (Many 'solutions' to the mind–body problem have this character, e.g. panpsychism.)

inseparability thesis is misplaced—perhaps this law of subjectivity has the same primitive status as it is tempting to
ascribe to the other laws of subjectivity I discussed in chapter
3. But if it is thus primitive, I would insist that it is not
philosophically trivial; it is an interesting and significant fact
about perception that it obeys this modal law.

These attempts at explanation have parallels in respect of
indexicals. Granted that indexical concepts are ineliminable
from direct cognitive awareness of the world, what is the
explanation of this? Is there some further feature of the
cognitive faculty concerned from which this ineliminability
can be derived? It is obvious that a medium theory would be
hopeless, since indexical properties are correctly ascribed to
objects and they contain genuine information; a use–mention
error theory is even less plausible in their case than in the
case of secondary qualities. But an analogue of the utility
theory looks more attractive; I shall call this the agency
theory. The agency theory, like the utility theory, locates the
raison d'être of indexicals in their practical role: they are
ineliminable because they are necessary for action. As I
remarked in chapter 5, indexicals have recently been
associated with practical reasoning, the thesis being that
indexical thought is a necessary condition of agency.[48] The
present suggestion, then, is that indexical concepts are ineliminable because without them agency would be impossible:
when I imagine myself divested of indexical thoughts,
employing only centreless mental representations, I *eo ipso*
imagine myself deprived of the power to act. I am inclined to
agree that indexical thought is essential to agency, but I doubt
that this can be the answer to our question about ineliminability. For the obvious question is whether it is possible for
a non-agent to be innocent of egocentric representations: if
indexical concepts still seem necessary to the thought of such
a purely contemplative being, then this indispensability
cannot be because such concepts are demanded by the

---

[48] See Perry, 'The Problem of the Essential Indexical'.

capacity to act. It is a difficult question whether the idea of
a conscious thinking being includes the idea of an agent, but
I think it is intuitively plain that indexical modes of presentation of space, time, oneself, etc. would be necessary even if
they did not feed into action. The connexion with agency
thus seems consequential rather than constitutive; the world
is presented to us indexically in advance of any connexion
with the will.[49] So the agency theory does not operate at the
right point: it tries to explain the essential role of indexical
awareness in terms of a connexion with something extrinsic
to that awareness. The agency theory of indexical ineliminability thus has the same sort of defect as the utility theory
of secondary quality ineliminability. What then about the
intentionality theory? Well, it does seem possible to make
parallel suggestions about the role of indexicals. As I have
said, in indexical thought the world is represented in a subject-
involving way; it is represented by way of certain relations to
oneself. Thus the mind makes a subjective contribution when
the indexical perspective is brought to bear, this perspective
interlocking with the presented objects in such a way as to
make them objects of thought. It seems, then, that we have
the same kind of structure as in the case of secondary qualities:
a coming together of a mind subjectively constituted in a
certain way and an objective world, where the mind establishes a direct cognitive relation to the world by dint of
subject-involving representations. Thus when I think of a
place as 'here' I bring it into relation to my subjective perspective as well as apprehending *it* in a certain way: the indexical
concept expressed by 'here' points, so to speak, in two directions. The intentionality theory will then say that indexical
concepts establish by this means a direct cognitive relation
to the world.[50] Such directness is not present in non-indexical

---

[49] That is, the relation of acquaintance *itself* requires mediation by indexical
modes of presentation; this is not a requirement externally imposed upon
acquaintance by the fact that we act upon the data of acquaintance. A purely
contemplative being with the faculty of direct cognitive awareness would still
represent the world from an indexical perspective.

[50] Depending upon the precise way in which indexical concepts are said to

thought, e.g. thought involving purely general definite descriptions; and the reason (it may be suggested) is that such thoughts do not employ the sorts of cognitive device which establish an immediate link between subject and object, i.e. concepts which 'use the subject to identify the object'. Again, I do not wish to assert this theory with any great confidence, though I think that it too has a certain intuitive force; I put it forward as worth considering. And I am open to the possibility that the ineliminability of indexicals might prove to be primitive, an inexplicable datum about the conditions of direct acquaintance in judgement. But on this somewhat inconclusive note I must leave the question of the explanation of the ineliminability theses.

It will have been apparent for some time now that the position I am advocating has a Kantian ring. Kant held that, contrary to what it is natural to believe, the form of our perceptual experience, in respect of space and time, has its source, not in how the world is constituted independently of the mind, but in the structure of the mind itself: the mind imposes its subjective categories on experience as an ineluctable necessity—or better, what it *is* to have perceptual experience is constituted by these subjectively founded categories.[51] Thus we perceive space as conforming to Euclidean geometrical laws, not because objective (noumenal) space satisfies those laws, but because the mind is so constructed as to impose those laws upon our perception of space. In short, and roughly, Kant assigned certain (allegedly) necessary features of experience to the intrinsic subjective

relate to the subject (see chapter 2) we will get different accounts of how the intentionality of indexical thoughts implicates the subject of those thoughts. Suppose we take the strongest variant of this egocentricity thesis, namely that all indexicals are *definable* in terms of 'I-now': then the intentionality theory will say that all indexical awareness consists (partly) in a direct awareness of oneself at the present time, so that the object of awareness is brought into relation with oneself as so presented. Non-indexical thought does not likewise represent its intentional object as standing in a relation to what is thus immediately presented to us, viz. ourselves. The idea then is that we are directly presented in indexical thought with things other than ourselves by virtue of their being (definitionally) related to an indexical whose reference is the directly presented self.

[51] Kant, *Critique of Pure Reason.*

constitution of the mind and not to an independently determinate reality which the mind merely passively reflects. My
own contentions have a similar form: I have claimed that
perceptual experience has certain necessary features—
notably that it represents objects in the world as having
secondary qualities—and that these features (contrary to
what might uncritically be supposed) owe their presence in
the content of experience to the subjective make-up of the
perceiver; it is not that the mind merely reflects what is
objectively there. Moreover, these necessary features of
experience themselves conform to certain laws—rather as
the necessary spatiality of experience, for Kant, conformed
to the Euclidean laws; I called these 'laws of subjectivity'
and argued for their *sui generis* character. This Kantian-
sounding conclusion results from combining three theses
about secondary qualities which are usually kept separate:
that they are subjective in nature; that they are inseparable
from experience of an objective world; that they display a
rich and irreducible set of quasi-logical laws. Putting these
theses together, we can say that *perceptual experience
necessarily represents the world subjectively* and that this
subjectivity brings its own laws. My general position differs
from a truly Kantian doctrine in that I also hold that experience succeeds in representing the world objectively, since
primary quality perceptual content is not contributed by the
mind—it reflects what is objectively present.[52] There is

---

[52] Kant, indeed, explicitly claims that primary qualities should be treated as
Locke treated secondary qualities, i.e. as powers to affect us in certain ways and
not as properties of 'things in themselves': see his *Prolegomena to any Future
Metaphysics*, First Part, Remark II. While I think this is an illuminating way to
understand Kant's account of the relation between appearance and reality (cf.
Putnam, *Reason, Truth and History*, pp. 60 ff.), it cannot be said that our
concepts of primary qualities offer any encouragement to Kant's extension of the
Lockean dispositional thesis to them. First, as I have repeatedly observed, we
acknowledge an intuitive distinction between (e.g.) shape and colour in respect
of their relation to sensory experience, a distinction which reflects a fundamental
difference in the satisfaction conditions of the corresponding predicates; and
second, in order that we have available an *explanation* of our perception of the
qualities of objects we need to be able to conceive primary qualities as consisting
in something other than powers to produce experiences: the Kantian extension
robs us of any means of explaining our perceptions in terms of properties of the

nothing noumenal about objective things on my view; we know them directly in experience. The difference between the world of appearance and the objective mind-independent world is not an ontological difference; it is a difference, I claimed, in the faculties through which a single world is represented. But despite this non-Kantian ingredient I think that my own contentions, if they be accepted, should, quite properly, induce the kind of impression of a changed perspective on one's experience which Kant aimed to bring about: for I think that the initial naive (though recognisably philosophical) view of secondary quality experience does take it to have essentially the same status as primary quality experience; and so acknowledging a deep difference between them, along with the consequences of that difference, should cause us to view our experience in a different way.[53] Reading Kant one gets the feeling of being imprisoned in one's own mind, constitutionally unable to shake off the subjective categories and apprehend the (noumenal) world as it is in itself. It would not be inappropriate, I think, to have some of the same feeling about sensory experience in respect of secondary qualities—the feeling that the very nature of experience precludes being perceptually presented with things just as they are in themselves. But this inescapable

object perceived (not that this bothered Kant). It is, in fact, crucial to the idea, that what appears to us in perception *is* just the mind-independent thing-in-itself, that primary qualities *not* be conceived as Lockean powers.

[53] I do not mean that *common sense* wrongly assimilates secondary to primary qualities, an assimilation that philosophical reflection confutes; in fact, I see no convincing reason to accuse common sense of any error as to the status of secondary qualities (see chapters 7 and 8). My point is that there is a natural *philosophical* tendency to award the same objective status to the two kinds of quality, which probably stems from elevating our customary unreflectiveness about the relativity of secondary qualities into a theory of their nature. If there is such a natural philosophical tendency, then my position belongs to that general category of philosophical positions which claim as the purest common sense what philosophers are prone vigorously to dispute. (Cf. Berkeley and Wittgenstein on the relationship between their philosophies and what is implicit in common-sense conceptions.) Distinguishing primary and secondary qualities can seem surprising and philosophically innovative, not because it conflicts with our ordinary common-sense concepts, but because (as well as articulating what those concepts implicitly contain) such a distinction cuts against a natural philosophical inclination to suppose there to be no important difference.

subjectivity is mitigated, as it was not for Kant, by the possi-bility of *conceiving* the world just as it objectively is.[54] In the next chapter I enquire into what makes this possible.

[54] Put in Kantian terminology, I do not hold that the 'understanding' is fettered by the same subjective constraints as 'intuition'; and it is important that this should be so, if we are to hope for a conception of the world as it is inde-pendently of the way it appears to us.

7
The Manifest Image
and the Scientific Image[1]

The world as it is presented to us in perception—the manifest image—includes secondary qualities; but the world as described by (physical) science is independent of this or that creature's perceptual peculiarities—it deals only in primary qualities. The exclusion by the scientific image of secondary qualities implies, by the considerations of chapter 6, that the scientific standpoint is not and cannot be a perceptual standpoint: the content of the scientific conception is not a possible (total) content of experience. Certainly we perceive some of the properties science ascribes to things, for we perceive primary qualities; but it is not possible to perceive *only* such qualities. Since perception is not a faculty through which it is possible to prescind from our subjective contribution, whereas the scientific image attempts to do precisely that, we cannot hope to make the content of scientific theories intelligible to ourselves by imagining, still less occupying, a perceptual standpoint embodying all and only the representations of the world offered by science: the scientific image is not an *image* at all.[2] To make sense of science, then, it seems that we need something more like the rationalists' idea of 'pure intellection'—a means of mental representation which is non-sensory in character.[3] Empiricists

[1] This terminology is Sellars's: see his 'Philosophy and the Scientific Image of Man'.
[2] We could put the point by saying that science aims for *neutrality* in its depiction of the world: it should not be possible to read off from a scientific theory any peculiarities of its propounder. But (as we have seen) the content of perceptual experience is necessarily *not* neutral, since it must represent the world as having properties which belong to it only in virtue of the peculiarities of the (type of) perceiver in question. It is a closely connected point that perception cannot represent the world as it is (entirely) *independently* of the perceiver —but just this is what a scientific description aspires to achieve.
[3] Thus Descartes insists upon a distinction between imagination and intellect, and associates theoretical understanding with the latter faculty, even holding that imagination may impede understanding: see Descartes, *Meditations,*

typically try to preserve their sensory theory of concepts by envisaging superior modes of perception in cases where human perceptual faculties give out; but it seems that the absolute conception cannot be accounted for in this way— its availability requires us to recognise a radical discontinuity between the conceptions of science and the representations of sense.[4] In a word, the 'ideas' of science are not to be construed as 'faint copies' of any *possible* 'impression'. This objection to empiricist accounts of scientific thought is in a way the reverse of the usual objection: the usual objection is that the contents of experience are *insufficient* to deliver the full content of scientific theories; the present objection is rather that experience is too *rich* in content, because too infused with subjective elements, to provide a basis for the austere objectivity of the scientific conception. This problem for empiricism results from supposing the absolute conception to be available to thought while acknowledging the full import of the Berkeley point; simple empiricism can be sustained only by rejecting one or other of these claims. The point can be put yet more starkly by remembering the relativity of perceptual content in respect of secondary qualities: conjoining this with the Berkeley point we see that perception is *necessarily* relative in its representational content, whereas the scientific image aims for absoluteness. Even the perceptions of God could not provide what the empiricist requires to meet this objection. Similar objections to empiricist epistemology have often been raised with regard to mathematical concepts and concepts of unobservables

VI. My present point, put in these terms, is that imagination must represent the physical world from the subjective point of view inherent in the perception of secondary qualities, whereas scientific understanding must prescind from this subjectivity and so requires an exercise of the intellect. The question of the need for, and possibility of, such a faculty of intellect is the crux of the disagreement between rationalists and empiricists, so if the present point is right the rationalists would seem to emerge victorious.

[4] Acknowledging such discontinuity seems to go against the spirit of Dummett's 'Common Sense and Physics': but the matter is clouded by the fact that Dummett does not distinguish the strictly *perceptual* point of view from the body of *beliefs* we call 'common sense'—and this latter may be regarded as continuous with science inasmuch as its *explanations* invoke only primary qualities.

(among others); the objection I am now putting applies even to the concepts often supposed most favourable to the empiricist, namely concepts of causal properties of macroscopic perceptible objects. To cope with this objection the empiricist must abandon any simple sensory account of how thought acquires conceptual content and move to some kind of abstractionism: this operation of abstraction directed upon sensorily presented material has the unpromising task of separating the secondary qualities from the primary qualities with which they are necessarily co-instantiated in experience. Berkeley appreciated the problem this raises clearly; and rejecting abstractionism he found the Lockean view of physical objects incoherent.[5] If you wish to preserve the Lockean view consistently with empiricism, then you must disagree with Berkeley's animadversions on abstraction; later in this chapter I shall return to the question of abstraction and the content of the absolute conception. For the moment it is enough to point out that the apparent discontinuity between the manifest image and the scientific image can be reduced only by recourse to something like a doctrine of abstractionism; it cannot be dissolved by the empiricist tactic of envisaging the possibility of superior perceivers. But before enquiring whether the scientific image might be derivable by abstraction from the manifest image, let me put two other questions: (a) how does the distinction between the two images arise? and (b) is there any conflict between them? In answering both questions it is essential to have a clear understanding of the nature of secondary qualities.

The perceptually based picture of objects is the one we are given, the one we start off with; the picture which results from prescinding from our subjective contribution is arrived

---

[5] See Berkeley's 'Introduction' to *The Principles of Human Knowledge*. In §10 of that work Berkeley applies his general rejection of abstract ideas to the special case of ideas of primary qualities in criticism of the Lockean conception of physical objects; in fact, the polemical force of the inseparability thesis, as Berkeley sees it, depends upon the correctness of his account of concepts. I shall agree with Berkeley about abstractionism, but draw a quite different conclusion from his.

at as a result of reflection, if it is arrived at at all. But what induces us so to detach our conception of perceptible objects from the perceptual point of view within which they are originally presented? What prompts us to form the idea of objects as they are in themselves, possessed only of primary qualities? One suggestion is that the secondary qualities are omitted as a consequence of empirical discoveries: science empirically discovered that secondary qualities are not needed to explain the interactions of things and that primary qualities are needed for this.[6] According to this view, there is no *a priori* reason why the two images should differ in content; it has merely *turned out* that the scientific image contains one sort of quality and not the other. We might say that, according to this view, it was epistemically possible that things should turn out to be red or sweet in themselves. It seems to me, however, that this is the wrong way to understand the distinction between the two images: I think it is an *a priori* truth that only the primary qualities correspond to how things are in themselves, and therefore *a priori* that the content of the two images is different. The key point is that it is an *a priori* matter whether some quality is primary or secondary, i.e. whether it is to be analysed in terms of a disposition to produce experiences: we can tell, by reflecting on the concepts, that (e.g.) red is secondary and square is primary—as is shown by our intuitions about the different relations in the two cases between seeming to have the quality and really having it.[7]

Now the dispositionality thus implicitly contained in certain

---

[6] This is a view I have often heard expressed in discussion. Jackson, for one, appears to accept it without question: see *Perception*, chap. 5.

[7] To say that it could not have turned out that red was a primary quality or that square was a secondary quality is not, of course, to say that it may not be a matter of *dispute* whether some given quality is primary or secondary—but the dispute is philosophical not scientific. Neither is it to deny that whether a property is explanatorily fundamental can be (typically is) an empirical question: and it *might* turn out that our common-sense primary qualities are not what we need to give an ultimate scientific explanation of how the world works. What is *a priori* is rather the relation of these perceptible qualities to experience. (It is an interesting and substantive question *why* it should be thus *a priori* whether a quality is primary or secondary; but I won't try to answer this question here.)

of our concepts of perceptible qualities has two consequences, noted earlier: that those concepts do not afford a *uniquely* correct description of the objects to which they apply, on account of the implied relativity; and that we cannot defensibly use those concepts to *explain* our perception of the qualities they pick out.[8] Thus ascribing 'red' to an object is relative and non-explanatory, whereas ascribing 'square' to an object is non-relative and explanatory. But the following propositions seem to me to be true: that there exists a non-relative description of any object, a single way it is in itself; and that we require a conception of the genuinely explanatory traits of an object. Secondary qualities cannot fulfil either of these requirements, but primary qualities can. We thus detach our conception of objects from their secondary qualities because we wish to have a unique and explanatory set of description of objects.[9] Since the notion of how things are in themselves seems bound up with these two conditions— uniqueness and explanatory power—and since we know *a priori* that secondary qualities cannot fulfil them, we inevitably arrive at the idea that objects in themselves have only primary qualities. The reason secondary qualities do not belong to the scientific image is therefore that they fail *a priori* to meet the conditions it demands. And given the Berkeley point, this implies that it is an *a priori* necessity that the manifest and scientific images possessed by any intelligent being should diverge in their content. I would say the same about indexical descriptions: they are originally given in our pre-scientific awareness of the world, and science must

[8] See chapter 2.

[9] Also we wish a conception of physical objects as existentially independent of us—a conception that permits us to say 'if no perceivers had existed, physical objects still would (or could) have'. But if we could not detach our conception of physical objects from their possession of subjectively constituted properties, then there would be a sense in which they could not exist unperceived—for they could not be conceived to lack properties whose possession depends upon the existence of perceivers. Resisting idealism thus requires us to reject the inseparability thesis as applied to conception—on pain of making the mind-independent world literally unconceivable. (I suppose this could be seen as a partial vindication of Berkeley's argument for idealism, scouted in chapter 6—in respect of its validity, not its soundness.)

prescind from them to fulfil its aims. But it would be absurd, I take it, to suggest that it has merely *turned out* that the laws of physics do not contain indexical concepts, as it has turned out that they do not contain (e.g.) the concept of phlogiston: surely the relativity and causal irrelevance of indexical properties unsuits them *a priori* to figure in the scientific image.[10] We cannot really suppose that there is some empirically possible physical theory which treats indexical properties as genuine explanatory states of the world, a body of physical laws in which indexicals play an essential role; nor, similarly, is there an empirically possible physical theory in which (what we now call) secondary qualities play the explanatory role actually played by primary qualities.

It has often been supposed that there is a conflict or disagreement between the common-sense view of objects associated with perception and the scientific view of them. The conflict is held to consist, roughly, in this: that common sense says that objects are coloured while science (or scientifically informed philosophy) tells us that they are not *really* coloured (and similarly for the other secondary qualities). Colour is ascribed to objects in the manifest image, but withheld or denied in the scientific image: common sense supposes colours to be really 'out there' qualifying physical objects, whereas science and critical philosophy teach that they are in fact only 'in the mind'.[11] This alleged conflict has been reacted to in a variety of ways, none of them altogether soothing. Some have concluded that common sense is in radical error, that perception itself is under an illusion as to the location of secondary qualities: science is right to deny

---

[10] I am not saying that indexical concepts could have no place in *any* set of explanatory principles, or even in any science: it seems likely, on the contrary, that psychology will require to employ indexical concepts in giving the content of causal-explanatory propositional attitudes. My point is rather that predication of indexical concepts of things in the world can have no scientific utility. (A similar point holds for secondary quality concepts: they may well have a use in the psychology of perception, in giving the content of experiences which themselves have a causal-explanatory role; but they have no explanatory utility as direct predications of objects.)

[11] I suppose the idea of this conflict goes back to Locke and beyond; the ancient atomists are often credited with raising the issue, at least in a primitive way.

that things are really coloured and common sense is simply mistaken in its assertion to the contrary.[12] Some have supposed that common sense and science speak of ontologically distinct worlds, the objects of the former being coloured, the objects of the latter not: neither view is in error about its own world—the only error lies in identifying the objects of each.[13] Others have wished to make common sense veracious by adopting an instrumentalist or fictionalist attitude toward science: common sense describes things as they really are, science merely offers a more or less useful picture of the world abstracted from common sense— science does not properly *deny* that things are coloured, because it does not *purport* to describe reality as it is in itself.[14] Then there are those who opt for a relativist view of colour-ascription: the conflict is resolved by acknowledging that ascriptions of qualities to objects are always made relatively to some chosen standpoint on the world. Relative to the perceptual standpoint things are really red, but relative to the scientific (or philosophical) standpoint they are not really red: so if we ask 'is the pillar box red?' no answer can be given until we specify which standpoint is to serve as standard.[15] And yet others seek to dissolve the disagreement by suggesting that common sense and science are in different lines of business: the purpose of science is theoretical knowlege of the world, but the purpose of common sense and perception is essentially practical; the conflict is resolved by saying that neither side wishes to usurp the role of the other.[16]

[12] Russell gives voice to this view in a well-known passage: 'Naive realism leads to physics, and physics, if true, shows that naive realism is false. Therefore naive realism, if true, is false; therefore it is false.' *An Inquiry into Meaning and Truth*, p. 13.

[13] Thus Eddington spoke of there being 'two tables', the table of science and the table of common sense: see *The Nature of the Physical World*. And Husserl seems to draw a similar conclusion from the Berkeley point: see *Ideas*, §40, p. 128.

[14] Thus Bradley, for example, speaks of the scientist's world of primary qualitied objects as a mere 'ideal construction' or 'fiction': see *Appearance and Reality*, p. 434. See also, for a critical discussion of this strategy, J. J. C. Smart, *Philosophy and Scientific Realism*, chap. IV.

[15] Strawson makes this suggestion in 'Perception and its Objects', §III.

[16] This is a view that can be read into what Descartes and Locke say about

My own view is that none of these strange and strained doctrines is needed because there is no real conflict between science and common sense as to whether things are really coloured. Firstly, it is not true that, according to the subjectivist view of colour (etc.), it is incorrect to ascribe colours to things; for they do indeed have the power to produce the appropriate sense-experiences in perceivers. What the scientifically informed view denies is just that objects are *objectively* or *intrinsically* coloured, i.e. that objects have colour in the way they have shape; it denies that possession of colour is an observer-independent condition. Now for there to be a conflict between science and common sense the latter would have to contradict this denial; it would have to hold, not just that things are really (i.e. truly) coloured, but further that they are objectively coloured—that being coloured is *not* observer-dependent. But is there any reason to convict common sense of the belief that secondary qualities have the same observer-independent status as primary qualities? I know of no feature of our ordinary use and understanding of colour words which clearly commits common sense to this mistaken assimilation. A bad argument for the allegation that common sense is thus in error is this: the correct analysis of 'red' is in terms of 'looks red', whereas such an analysis is not correct for 'square'; but we do not, in ordinary talk, make this difference explicit by saying that things (merely) *look* red but *are* square—we do not actually employ the correct analysans of 'red'. But of course this does not show that common sense refrains from acknowledging the dispositional analysis, still less that it rejects this analysis. It would, indeed, not be wrong of us to employ the analysans instead of the analysandum in ordinary situations, but our refraining from doing so does not indicate any repudiation of the analysis. First, given the way things are, explicitly to employ the analysans would carry unwanted conversational implicatures, to the effect that the perceptual conditions are

theoretical and practical knowledge of the world: see Descartes, *Meditations*, VI; Locke, *Essay, passim.*

abnormal in some way.[17] Second, the 'looks red' locution is such as to permit semantic detachment of 'red', so that it can always be predicated of objects just as it is: so even speakers who *explicitly* acknowledged the analysis in their colour ascriptions would still be committed to the independent semantic significance of 'red'. Third, it is absurd to require, as a condition of the veracity of common sense, that it always replace any concept by its correct philosophical analysis: no-one (I take it) would suggest that common sense is in error about the concept of knowledge because it does not replace that concept with its correct philosophical analysis (supposing it to have one). So there is no ground here for convicting common sense of objectivising secondary qualities.

A *prima facie* better argument starts from the observation that our words for primary and secondary qualities have the same grammatical or logical form: both 'red' and 'square' are monadic predicates of objects. But, it may be said, the relativity of colour ascription amounts to the claim that colour predicates conceal an extra argument-place for a perceiver or group of perceivers: to be red consists in presenting a certain appearance to certain perceivers, so that the 'real nature' of this quality is best revealed by a dyadic predicate 'red(x,y)'; whereas this would be wrong for 'square'. Put baldly, the accusation is that ordinary language, and so common sense, treats as a property what is really a relation: it treats 'red' like 'square' and thus invites the charge of mistaken objectification.[18] However, this argument is unpersuasive because it is common for relational properties to be represented in speech by means of monadic predicates. Consider 'nourishing', 'frightening', 'attractive', 'lethal': these words are commonly used as monadic predicates, but brief reflection on how things are with different species of animal

[17] Cf. Grice's discussion of the conversational implicatures of the 'looks' locution in 'The Causal Theory of Perception'.

[18] That is, by treating 'red' as an *absolute* predicate of objects common sense implicitly rejects the relativity of colour ascriptions to perceivers.

shows that they stand for relational properties. This disparity between ordinary speech and correct analysis does not, however, lead us to think that common sense is in *error* about what it is for something to be (e.g.) nourishing—that it mistakes this for an intrinsic property of things. The reason the relativity is not explicitly signalled in ordinary talk is that the intended reference class (e.g. human beings) is normally evident from the context; the relativity would soon enough be made explicit if this were not clear from the context. Similarly, our ascriptions of colour typically take place against the background of an assumed reference class of normal human perceivers, so that the monadic form is tacitly understood as relative to that class; but our speech would be deprived of this convenience if the assumed conditions changed. Suppose Martians became integrated into human society and that they looked just like human beings, despite the systematic difference of their colour vision. Then communication with them about the colours of things would require an explicit indication of reference class: we would have to say of pillar boxes that they are red for human beings but green for Martians—if someone just said that pillar boxes are red *tout court* his interlocutor would not know what to expect when he looked at a pillar box. I think, therefore, that the syntactic similarity of 'red' and 'square' does not show that common sense (wrongly) regards colour as non-relational.

But does common sense actually endorse the relational view of secondary qualities? It seems to me that it does, simply because the dispositional account of such qualities is derivable *a priori* from the content of the corresponding concepts. If the distinction between primary and secondary qualities, in respect of their observer-dependence, were an empirical distinction, then our ordinary concepts would not register the difference of status of the qualities; but since the demarcation can be made *a priori* it is implicit in common sense concepts that colour is observer-dependent and hence subjective. This is not, of course, to say that the 'ordinary man' holds the correct philosophical theory of colour: but it is to say that if he allows his philosophical reflections to be shaped by the concepts he actually uses, then he will come to hold that theory. Nor am I denying that there is a naive philosophical tendency to dispute the subjectivity of secondary qualities; but this is a philosophical naivety not a common sense one. The impression of discovery which attends making the primary/secondary distinction indicates no departure from common sense, since it results from reflection on the ordinary concepts; the departure is rather from a naive philosophical theory.[19] If this is right, then science and common sense do not in fact conflict over the question whether objects are really coloured: science allows that objects are really (i.e. truly) coloured but denies that they are objectively coloured; common sense likewise holds that it is external things that have colour, but it does not make the mistake of claiming that this is an objective matter. The appearance of conflict arises because of equivocation with the word 'really': it is used equivocally to mean 'truly' and 'objectively' in the original claim of incompatibility—distinguish these senses of 'really' and the apparent conflict dissolves.[20]

I do not take this irenical line out of a general desire to reconcile science and common sense; I would not, for example, hold that there is no conflict on the question of solidity. The word 'solid' has a number of distinct meanings, one of which is that of being materially dense or continuous in structure—being solid in this sense is a matter of having no internal cavities or interstices. Now it seems to me obvious

[19] Cf. chapter 6, note 53.

[20] In 'Common Sense and Physics' Dummett puts forward a related view about how the impression of conflict arises: he accuses those who stage a conflict of confusing two senses of the word 'appearance' (or of failing to distinguish two sorts of implication which the use of this word may carry): there is the sense which implies the commission of an actual error, and there is the sense which merely signals a relativity to our specific modes of sensory receptivity. And from the fact that a quality belongs to the realm of appearance in the relativity sense it does not follow that its ascription is erroneous. Just as 'really' can be used to mean either 'truly' or 'objectively', so 'apparently' can be used to mean either 'not truly' or 'relative to our specific sensitivities'.

that, as science has shown, ordinary material objects are not solid in this sense: they have a discontinuous granular structure and are full of cavities—this is just what the modern atomic theory of matter tells us; so if common sense contradicted this it would be in error. The question is whether common sense *does* believe that medium sized dry goods are solid in this sense. And it seems to me that there are grounds for saying that it does have this false belief. Let us define a common-sense belief to be (roughly) a belief which it is natural to have on the basis of how things look (or otherwise seem) to you in a suitably wide range of conditions. Now I think it is reasonable to claim that material things do *look* solid to us—a metal sphere looks to the human eye as if it were materially dense, i.e. devoid of internal cavities or surface granulations; and it also feels that way. We might say that such an object looks and feels just as it would were it, contrary to what is in fact the case, really solid: if the atomic theory were false and matter were really structurally continuous, then it would look just as it does now. Suppose half the objects of perception were solid and half were not, though we perceivers were not apprised of this; then I think it would be entirely natural, given the character of one's visual and tactual experience, to believe that all these objects were solid—for they all *look* solid.[21]   But this natural belief

[21] Note that I am here just *defining* a common-sense belief to be one whose content matches that of an associated experience: if something looks F, then the common-sense belief it is natural to have (in this defined sense) is that the thing is F. This is not to say that other 'common-sense' beliefs may not justify one in refraining from forming a belief in this way: you might, for example, know that looking F in the current circumstances is likely to be a perceptual illusion, and so you refrain from believing the perceived object to be F. In the case of solidity the inhibiting collateral belief may be that things could have cavities which are too small to see or feel: a judicious believer may not, then, believe that things are solid on the basis of how they look, and his restraint might reasonably be described as an exercise of common sense. I am not at all sure to what extent we can legitimately protect common sense from error by allowing such beliefs to overrule the data of perception—in particular, I am not sure whether these considerations show it to be wrong to ascribe a belief in the solidity of material things to 'pre-scientific man'. However, for my purposes it does not really matter how we resolve this question, for my primary claim is just that science has in this regard contradicted how things *look* and *feel* to us, rather than the beliefs we may or may not form on the basis of these sensory appearances. Common-sense *belief*

would be false. Compare the case of solidity with that of the shape of the earth: I would say that science contradicted common-sense belief with respect to the earth's shape. Given the way the earth looks from our position on its surface, it is natural to believe that the earth is flat: it looks just as it would look if it were flat, and ordinary observation is not able to disconfirm this belief. Or consider the revision of common-sense belief regarding the distribution of organisms which was brought about by the invention of the microscope. Ordinary pond water looks free of living organisms, so it is natural to believe that it is so; but this common-sense belief is shown to be false when the water is examined under a microscope. There is nothing mysterious about these cases; they simply bring out the fact that our senses may not have the acuity to detect how the world really is. Just as pond water looks not to harbour living organisms to the naked eye, so a metal sphere looks to the naked eye not to have a granular structure. Scientific theories and instruments of observation have thus falsified certain common-sense beliefs formed on the basis of how things look. So I think that solidity differs from redness in that (a) science actually denies outright that things are solid, and (b) common sense actually asserts that things are solid in precisely the sense in which science denies it. It is crucial to this difference between the two cases that solidity is not a secondary quality—that is, that being solid does not consist in looking solid in normal conditions. For, of course, if it were so definable, then science could not contradict the beliefs about solidity naturally formed as a result of perception. The appearance of solidity which things present is correctable by science only because solidity is the *sort* of quality to attach to things independently of how they strike perceivers; and this is why how things look under microscopes can undermine unaided

may perhaps be, in one sense, neutral on the question of solidity, but perceptual *experience* is, I think, firmly committed on the question: things do *look* solid, as the earth looks flat. My point is that these cases contrast with secondary quality perception in that they involve an erroneous perception whereas (e.g.) looking red is perfectly veridical.

perceptual ascriptions of solidity. It is different with secondary qualities: their ascription cannot be revised as a result of scientific theory or superior perceptual sensitivity because what it is to have them is just a matter of how things seem from a particular perceptual point of view. If grass looked a different colour under the microscope we would not conclude that grass is not really green; but if something looks gappy under a microscope we conclude that it is not really solid. To call something solid is to make a claim about how it is in itself, independently of the reactions of perceivers; whereas to call something red precisely is to make a claim about how it looks to certain perceivers. And it is in virtue of this difference that science and common sense conflict in the former case but not in the latter. This is why I said that in deciding whether the manifest and scientific images conflict it is essential to be clear whether one is dealing with a primary quality or a secondary quality.[22]

I earlier raised the question of whether the scientific image can be given a sensory interpretation: that is to say, whether the absolute conception of the world in which secondary qualities do not figure can be construed in terms of the content of some actual or possible perceptual experience. I said that this seemed impossible if the sensory interpretation consisted in the possibility of our having or imagining a form of experience in which only primary qualities are perceived. Berkeley concluded from this sort of consideration (in effect) that the absolute conception is incoherent, because of his empiricist constraints on the intelligibility of a putative conception of the world; I would prefer to abandon Berkeley's empiricist constraints and construe the content of the absolute conception in a non-sensory way. But as I noted earlier, there is a second way in which a sensory interpretation might

[22] In discussing the alleged conflict between science and common sense Strawson, for example, does not bother to distinguish the issue as it applies to primary and to secondary qualities: see his 'Perception and its Objects', § 111. His relativistic reconciliation seems to me to involve illicitly generalising a basically correct treatment of the case of secondary qualities to all qualities for which a conflict has been supposed.

be defended, namely by appeal to the mental operation of abstraction. The idea will be that we can form a conception of a purely primary qualitied object by discriminative attention to the primary qualities presented in experience, these being mentally separated from their secondary quality accompaniments. It thus seems that a sensory interpretation of the scientific image will perforce have recourse to an abstractionist theory of concept formation—empiricism requires abstractionism. Now abstractionism is a notoriously infirm theory in many respects, but I think it encounters a special difficulty in the present context.[23] One standard kind of objection to the doctrine is that many concepts simply do not correspond to distinguishable elements of experience—so it is with, e.g., number concepts and logical concepts. This is not, however, the problem with abstracting primary qualities—for they do correspond to presented elements of experience; the problem is rather their necessary inseparability from the qualities with which they are co-instantiated. The point is essentially Berkeley's: conceptual separation of an element of experience from other elements requires a mental operation of *detachment*; but this is impossible in respect of primary qualities—we cannot have a *sensory* idea of shape independently of some idea of colour (or a secondary quality of some other sense). The point here is not just the general criticism that abstractionism tries to treat qualities of objects as (detachable) parts, nor is it just the converse of the impossibility of abstracting colour from shape: there is a special failing of abstractionism as a theory of the content of the absolute conception. In the case of abstracting colour from shape it would not be obviously disastrous for the theory if the vestiges of an associated primary quality, so to speak, clung on to the abstracted colour—present in the sensory image but ignored for purposes of thought involving colour concepts. But if the abstractionist theory is introduced as a way of delivering a *purely* objective conception of things,

[23] For a general discussion of the problems of abstractionism see Geach, *Mental Acts*, §§6–12.

then this is a decisive objection: for if vestiges of associated secondary qualities cling on to the abstracted primary quality concept, then it cannot be said that abstractionism yields the desired purely objective conception. That is, Berkeley's objection has a special force when abstraction is required to divest a concept of all associations with certain other concepts: even if we agreed that a concept of squareness could consist in a quasi-sensory mental content with some associated colour, such a concept could not serve as part of the content of the absolute conception. So for general reasons, as well as for this special reason, I do not think it possible to construe the absolute conception as derived from sensory presentations by any mental operation of abstraction; and so I conclude that it cannot be given a sensory interpretation at all.[24]

I do not have an alternative theory of how the concepts of the scientific image are come by, but it does seem to me that a more rationalist epistemology is indicated by the above considerations: the manufacture of concepts must be thought of as the province of more intellective faculties of mind. The condition for being capable of an observer-independent conception of the world will then be that you can employ primary quality concepts in judgements other than those made in direct response to experience. We originally apply concepts of shape (etc.) to objects presented in perception, but if this were the *only* way in which those concepts could be exercised an objective conception would not be available to us: we think of the world purely objectively when we

[24] I am not, of course, suggesting that a theory which has objective content cannot be *verified* on the basis of subjective sensory data; I am speaking rather of the nature of the concepts which comprise the *content* of the theory. (I do think, though, that a verificationist account of scientific theories is cast into doubt by these considerations, since the materials it allows itself in accounting for these concepts are of an essentially sensory character.) We need a conception of primary qualities which is independent of the idea of what it would be to *perceive* their instantiation; but this is quite compatible with the recognition that statements ascribing such non-sensory qualities can be *tested* by observing (by sense) whether the quality is instantiated, since inherently non-sensory concepts are observably applicable to the objects of perception. (Cf. Evans's suggestive discussion of primary quality concepts, 'Things Without the Mind', Part III.)

employ primary quality concepts in judgements which are not made in response to what is perceptually presented—but in the formulation of physical laws and the like. Concepts suited to the objective conception are thus neither derived from, nor restricted in their application to, the contents of experience.

If I were asked to choose between the manifest image and the scientific image on the score of representational superiority, I would answer as follows: there is no clear sense in which one has greater verisimilitude than the other. The objective view does not have the relativity of the subjective view, but it purchases this absoluteness at the cost of removing itself from the perceptual standpoint. There can be no question of selecting one kind of view and abandoning the other: to abandon the subjective view is to abandon the possibility of experience of the world; to abandon the objective view is to abandon the idea of an observer-independent unitary reality. Neither view can serve the purposes of the other, and neither can be construed as setting a standard which the other can be criticised for failing to meet.

8
Other Issues

I should like in this final chapter to make some brief remarks on three issues involving secondary qualities; the issues are not (except perhaps for the first) directly related to the main theme of this essay, but they require a clear view of the nature of secondary qualities if they are to be given proper treatment. We may therefore regard the discussion of these issues as an application of results already arrived at. The issues are: whether a subjectivist theory of secondary qualities, in particular colour, requires rejection of a naive realist view of the immediate objects of perception; whether perception of secondary qualities raises special problems for physicalism; and whether it is helpful to compare moral values with secondary qualities. I begin with the question of naive realism, a question that has probably been troubling some readers from the outset.

(i) *Naive realism and secondary qualities.* By 'naive realism' I mean the view that the immediate objects of perception— those items we perceive but not in virtue of perceiving any- thing else—are material objects or their surfaces. The denial of this view is what is usually called a representational theory of perception (hereafter RTP): this theory holds that the immediate objects of perception are mental items ('sense- data'), and that material objects are perceived derivatively upon perception of these items.[1] So RTP as I shall under- stand it says that, contrary to what we ordinarily believe,

---

[1] I follow custom in calling this the 'representational' theory of perception. But I think the custom is unfortunate in its suggestion that one who holds (as I do) that experiences may be said to have representational (i.e. intentional) content is *eo ipso* committed to rejecting a naive realist view of perception: my position is rather that we see objects 'directly' *by* representing them in visual experience. For a recent statement of the kind of 'representational' theory I am going to discuss (and reject) see Jackson, *Perception.*

when you look at a pillar box the red thing you immediately
see is, not the (surface of the) pillar box, but an intermediate
mental sense-datum. Now the question I want to ask is
whether a subjectivist view of colour, such as I have adopted
in this essay, implies this theory of perception. It is very
often supposed that there is this implication, so that subjectivism about colour contradicts naive realism as formulated
above. However, I know of no extant argument which seems
to me even to get close to demonstrating any such entailment.
But in an effort to quiet doubts on the question I shall review
some arguments that have been offered, beginning with the
crudest and working up to something more challenging.

The crudest argument trades upon the idea that secondary qualities are 'in the mind' and not 'in objects': either
a quality is in the mind or it is in the object; secondary
qualities are not in objects, so they are in the mind; they
must then be instantiated by mental items; but whatever
item it is that has the secondary qualities is also (i.e. is
identical with) the item that has the primary qualities; so the
object of sight which looks red and round is really itself in
the mind; so RTP is true.[2] The main error of this argument
occurs in the first premiss: it is supposed that if a quality
is properly analysed by reference to something mental,
then it must be a quality *of* something mental—hence it is
not 'in the object'. The argument turns on ambiguity in the
phrase 'in the mind': this can mean either 'analysed by
reference to something mental' or 'correctly predicated
of something mental'; the mistake is to think that the former
entails the latter. Compare the property of being frightening:
this property is 'in the mind' in the first sense, but obviously
not in the second sense. What encourages the *non sequitur* is
an inability or unwillingness to grasp the irreducible

---

[2] Berkeley does seem guilty of reasoning this way, as I observed in chapter 6.
It is often supposed that Locke's 'representational' theory of perception is (in
part) derived from similar reasoning: however, recent work by Michael Ayers
(unpublished) has persuaded me that it is doubtful that Locke held RTP in the
form in which that theory is commonly ascribed to him, and so we cannot suppose
him to have argued to RTP in this sense from his doctrine of secondary qualities.

dispositionality of secondary qualities: they are dispositions *of objects* to produce *experiences*.

A second (closely related) argument relies upon the principle that if an object has a mental property it must be a mental object, this conjoined with the claim that (e.g.) colour is a mental property. Now it is not exactly false to say that being red is a mental property; for it is a property which things have only in relation to minds—'red' holds of things only in virtue of certain experiential facts. But it is fallacious to infer that the things of which it holds are themselves mental, i.e. do not also instantiate intrinsically non-mental properties such as shape. The point is that an object can be, so to speak, mental under one description and material under another: that is, the same item can have both mental and material attributes. This is indeed a banal claim, as the property of being frightening again bears out. Berkeley did reason in this fallacious way, aided by a suspect and tendentious use of 'in the mind'; but a correct subjectivist analysis of secondary qualities does not invite these inferences.[3]

The next argument is explicitly offered by certain contemporary writers.[4] This type of argument does not *start* with the subjective character of secondary qualities, as the previous ones do; it derives RTP by elimination, after showing that secondary qualities are not genuinely properties of material objects. The leading idea is that a scientifically informed conception of physical objects does not ascribe secondary qualities to them, since these are causally inefficacious and not part of an objective description of things;

---

[3] This Berkeleian argument is distinct from the pevious one. The previous one moves directly from the subjectivity of secondary qualities to the claim that mental items are the bearers of perceptible qualities; the present argument tries to show the subjectivity of all qualities, including primary qualities, on the basis of the principle that what is necessarily co-instantiated with a subjective quality must itself be a subjective quality. The second argument is easily assimilated to the first because its plausibility (such as it is) derives from tacitly assuming that secondary qualities are borne by mental items.

[4] See Jackson, *Perception*, esp chap. 5; and Armstrong, 'Perception, Sense Data and Causality', esp. §IV. I think that the line of thought these writers make explicit has been very influential in recommending RTP to philosophers of perception: cf., e.g., Russell's 'Sense Data and Physics'.

yet *something* must be (really) red, since that is how the objects of perception appear; so it must be that there are items distinct from material objects which bear these non-scientific qualities; and by elimination these must be mental. The weakness of this argument is clearly its assumption that all genuine properties of things are scientific properties; for only on this assumption is it possible to force the intro-duction of intermediate items to bear the non-scientific properties. But what about the host of other non-scientific dispositional properties of material things—being frighten-ing, beautiful, funny, interesting, etc.? Surely it would be absurd to introduce intermediate mental items to bear *these* properties just because they do not belong in the scientific description of ordinary material things. As I have said before, there is nothing to prevent one and the same object being presented, though in different ways, both to the scientific image and to the manifest image. The underlying mistake is to think that science has somehow *corrected* our common-sense ascription of secondary qualities to external things.[5]

The best argument I have been able to construct is structur-ally parallel to the one just rejected, but does not rely upon the assumption that the only genuine properties of material things are their scientific properties; and it may be that this is an argument which articulates the intuitive conviction many people have that a subjectivist account of secondary quali-ties puts us in peril of RTP. I think the argument fails, but it does bring out something interesting about the perception of secondary qualities. According to the dispositional analysis, an object is red if and only if (roughly) it looks red to some perceiver(s); being red is thus a relational property. But consider the phenomenology of our perception of red objects: it seems that when an object looks red it *looks* to have a monadic or intrinsic property—the phenomenological content of the experience seems to have the same *structure*

---

[5] Perhaps I should note that Jackson's (ibid.) version of the argument here rejected has a number of complexities I have not gone into; however, I cannot see that the complexities get around the basic objection I have lodged.

as when a square object is perceived. So we have a phenomenological symmetry between primary and secondary
quality perception but an analytic asymmetry, since the
former qualities are in their nature monadic and intrinsic
while the latter are not. We could put the point this way: for
an object to be red is for it to look red, but when something
looks red to a perceiver it does not *look* such as to look red
to some perceiver (say a human being). Thus, it may be said,
red objects do not look the way they are analysed as being by
the dispositional theory; they look the way they would look
if they were analysable as primary qualities are, i.e. non-
relationally. This apparent mismatch between the way a colour
quality looks and the way it inherently is, according to the
dispositional theory, thus seems to present us with three alter-
natives: either we admit that secondary quality experience
commits an error; or we give up the dispositional analysis; or we
suppose that what is immediately perceived is not (identical
with) the item which has the quality dispositionally, viz. the
material object. We do not want to take the first option,
since this convicts the necessary character of experience of a
radical error; and neither do we want to give up the dispositional theory. Therefore (the argument continues) we
must allow that *something* perceived as red is monadically or
intrinsically red; but we know that this cannot be the material
object; so we must introduce an intermediate entity to be the
bearer of intrinsic redness—which, by elimination, will be a
mental entity. On the resulting account of perception what is
going on when something looks red is the following: the
material object has a disposition to cause experiences as of
something looking intrinsically red; this red-looking item is
not the object itself but a sense-datum—so when we say a
material object looks red we really mean (or must mean) that
it is disposed to produce a *sense-datum* object which is
(intrinsically) red. On this account, there is no error in
experience, since the immediate object of perception has the
property of being red in just the way it seems to; and the
dispositional account of what it is for a *material* object to be

red is preserved—we thus avoid both perceptual error and repudiation of the dispositional analysis by adopting RTP.[6]

This argument has a sophistical feel, but wherein resides its mistake? I think that the way to rebut the argument is to deny that mismatch between phenomenology and analysis entails error—either perceptual or philosophical. That is, I agree that objects are not represented perceptually as being the way the correct analysis of secondary qualities asserts, but I do not think that this implies that the way things look is unveridical. The general principle I would appeal to here is that it is possible for a concept C to be analysable in terms of a condition A without it following that if it looks as if C is satisfied it must look as if A holds. The reason this principle is correct is that 'looks . . .' is a highly intensional context: we cannot substitute even analytic equivalences in its scope. The argument for RTP rested upon the thought that things do not in looking red look as the dispositional analysis asserts; but this is to assume that it is legitimate to substitute the dispositional analysis of 'red' inside the 'looks' context, and there is no reason to expect that such a substitution will preserve truth. We can truth-preservingly replace 'red' by its dispositional analysis when it occurs as a simple predicate of objects (as well as in modal contexts) but we cannot do so when it occurs after 'looks'. This no more implies error on the part of experience than the non-substitutability of analytic equivalents in speech act contexts implies error: it clearly does not follow from the fact that when a person says something containing the word 'know' he does not *say* what an analysis of 'know' might specify, either that the analysis is wrong or that the speaker is committing an error; similarly, the fact that 'looks' does not sustain substitution of analytic equivalences shows neither that experience is in error nor that the putative analysis is incorrect. So we do not need to resort to RTP to rescue perception of secondary qualities

---

[6] We secure the consequence that the item that looks square is not the material object by way of the principle that what looks square is identical with what looks red.

from error. This general point is obvious enough for empirical property reductions *vis-à-vis* how things look: we cannot substitute 'H_2O' for 'water' in 'looks like water', but this does not imply either that the reduction is wrong or that experience misleads us——I am saying that it is the same with the philosophical analysis of secondary qualities. Compare the perception of (say) politeness: suppose it is held, plausibly enough, that being polite consists in a certain relation between the agent's behaviour and the attitudes of members of some community——polite behaviour is the kind that is approved by members of a given community. Now consider how things look when someone behaves politely: it does not *look* as if the person is acting in a way approved of by a particular society; this is not how it seems phenomenologically. In this case we again have a 'mismatch' between how the behaviour is perceived and what it is analysed as, but there is surely no question here of error in how things look; and the reason is the intensionality of the 'looks' locution. Or again, it seems a misguided criticism of (say) Gricean analyses of meaning to insist that such analyses commit the perception of speech to error, on the ground that when a person hears an utterance as meaning such-and-such he does not *hear* it as uttered with the intention to produce in the audience the belief that the speaker believes that such-and-such by way of the audience's recognition of that intention.[7] For perceptual verbs simply do not in general permit substitution of analytic equivalents. We can therefore agree that secondary qualities do not look the way they are analysed as being, but point out that this does not imply that secondary quality experience is unveridical.[8] There is thus no obstacle to identifying the object that is dispositionally red with the object that looks intrinsically red.

[7] Grice, 'Meaning'. For both this case and the case of secondary qualities we can also make the point that philosophical analysis need not be construed as the production of synonyms: we are trying to spell out what certain facts consist in, rather than give an ordinary language equivalent of the terms being analysed. Viewed in this light, it becomes less surprising that philosophical analyses do not substitute into intensional contexts in which their analysandum occurs.

[8] I must confess to a residual uneasiness about this rebuttal of the argument, however. My worry can be put in terms of the scope of negation in perceptual

Indexicals provide a useful analogue for the above points. We can see clearly how mistaken would be the 'in the mind' argument for a representational theory of the objects of indexical thought, and the wrongness of introducing an intermediate mental object as the bearer of these subjective properties. Neither does it seem even momentarily enticing to move from the non-scientific character of indexical properties to the conclusion that it is not ordinary external things but inner mental items that are the immediate objects of indexical thought. And indexical ascriptions illustrate

statements as this bears upon the question of perceptual error. Suppose we have analysed a concept C by means of a condition A; then two sorts of mismatch with perception of the satisfaction of C are possible: either it does not seem to be the case that A is met when C is perceived to be satisfied; or it seems to be the case that A is *not* met when C is perceived to be satisfied. Now it may be said that I have made it plausible that the first case is not incompatible with analysing C as A—so that analysing 'red' as 'looks red to x' is compatible with its being the case that when something looks red it does not look to have such a relational property—but it is a further question whether the second kind of case has been satisfactorily dealt with—i.e. the (apparent) fact that a red thing looks *not* to be relationally red. The first thing I would say to this is that the way in which negation contributes toward specifying the content of experience when it has narrow scope with respect to a perceptual verb is very unclear: in particular, it is unclear whether in order that something looks not-ϕ to someone the question of its being ϕ has to have arisen in the person's mind (does it look to me that it is not the case that there are elephants in this room if I have not considered the question?). Secondly, I am not at all sure that it is really right to say of someone looking at a red object that it looks *non*-relationally red to him, as distinct from its not looking relationally red; for this seems to require more sophistication in the content of the experience than is strictly warranted. Compare the perception of motion: we know that all motion is relative, but it is also true that we do not perceive the motion of objects *as* relative to our own motion as the earth rotates. Should we say, more strongly, that we perceive the motion of (say) a ball *not* to be relative to the motion of the earth? This seems too much; and I think it not unreasonable to suggest that the same is true of the relativity of secondary qualities: shifting negation from wide to narrow scope seems to require the presence of a thought, on the part of the perceiver, which if it is not plausible to ascribe to him in normal perceptual circumstances. If this is right, then our perceptual experience does not strictly *contradict* the relational character of secondary qualities (and motion); but the questions raised here could stand further investigation. What makes me uneasy with this response is that there seemed *something right* in the idea, exploited by the argument for RTP, that objects look *intrinsically* red. If we take this idea seriously, then we *may* be forced to escape RTP by admitting (unappealingly) to a certain kind of error in perception: not indeed the error of ascribing colours to material objects, but the error of regarding these qualities of objects as intrinsic rather than relational. (What one would really *like* to say here is that something can seem not-ϕ and be in fact ϕ, and yet for this not to rate as a straightforward perceptual *illusion*.)

how representational content can have a monadic structure though it consists fundamentally in something relative: thus, for example, when I say that an object is 'here' I ascribe an inherently relational property in a monadic form; but I commit no error in failing to make explicit the relativity to myself. No-one would think that indexical thought is not immediately of external non-mental objects on the ground that such objects have indexical properties in a relative way whereas the objects of indexical thought are conceived under monadic concepts—as here, now, me, etc.[9]

I conclude, then, that naive realism about the objects of perception is not threatened by the subjectivist theory of secondary qualities.

(ii) *Physicalism and secondary qualities.* I think there are two levels at which mental states directed onto secondary qualities pose a greater challenge to a broadly physicalist view of the mind than mental states directed onto primary qualities—namely, the level of thought and the level of experience. At the level of thought, the difference comes from the more intimate connexion between possession of secondary quality concepts and sensory consciousness than that between possession of primary quality concepts and such consciousness. As T. Nagel has emphasised, facts about how things subjectively seem—experiential facts—confront physicalism with an especially intractable problem; so if a certain kind of concept depends for its possession upon the enjoyment of specific sorts of sensory experience, then thoughts involving such concepts will inherit the

---

[9] However, I think that the fact that in the case of indexicals we have a monadic representation of what is really a relative condition does not quite mirror what is troublingly true of the perceptual representation of secondary qualities and their fundamental nature: for it seems that the self to which the indexical is relative does enter into the indexical thought in a way that the perceiver does not enter the content of his experience—one thinks of something as here 'for me', but one does not see something as red 'for me' (we do not want to say that the visual perceiver always visually represents himself). So it would be misguided to press the analogy in order to relieve the anxieties expressed in the previous footnote.

physicalistically problematic character of the corresponding experiences.[10] My claim then is that secondary quality concepts depend for their possession upon experience of secondary qualities, whereas primary quality concepts can be possessed in logical independence of the enjoyment of specific sensory experiences.[11] This is really just another way of putting an old doctrine: that a man born blind cannot have the concept of red, but there is no (sense-specific) experience such that lack of it precludes possessing the concept of squareness—indeed, this concept could (logically) be possessed by a being entirely lacking sense experience. Put differently, Martians with different senses from ours, or no senses at all, could understand our scientific theories, but they could not grasp our concepts of secondary qualities or the laws of subjectivity they obey. The reason for this difference stems directly from the different relation the two kinds of quality have to experience: to grasp what it is to be red is to know the kind of sensory experience red things produce, given the subjectivist analysis of this secondary quality; but it is not true that to grasp what it is to be square one needs to know what kinds of sensory experience

[10] Nagel, 'What is it like to be a bat?' Nagel writes as if the property of subjectivity he wishes to isolate applies only to 'experiences' and not to propositional attitudes; indeed he sometimes suggests that intentional states are in principle ascribable to a (non-conscious) computer: see 'Subjective and Objective', p. 201. One might justify this difference of attitude by observing that there is nothing it is like to have a concept—possessing a concept is not a phenomenological state. If this is what lies behind Nagel's divided attitude, then I think he is quite right: but it does not follow that possessing concepts is logically independent of the enjoyment of mental states which *do* have Nagel's subjectivity property (I do not say that Nagel thinks it does). My point is that, while there is indeed nothing it is like, phenomenologically, to possess the concept *red*, it is nevertheless true that possessing this concept logically requires the enjoyment of experiences as of red things. So some propositional attitudes do (albeit indirectly) introduce the problem for physicalism that Nagel attributes to experiences: thoughts about red things are thus not available to insentient computers, even if other types of thoughts may be (I am not asserting that they are).

[11] It is worth noting that geometrical concepts, in particular, have often been regarded as *a priori* concepts just in the sense that they can be possessed 'independently of experience'; secondary quality concepts are *a posteriori* according to this definition. Putting the distinction this way provides a sense in which the rationalists were right to insist that genuinely scientific knowledge consists of *a priori* concepts.

square things produce, since such a disposition is not *constitutive* of what it is to be square.[12] Given the principle that concepts of sensory experience are graspable only if one is acquainted with the experience in question, we thus have the result that secondary quality concepts can be possessed only if one is acquainted with certain kinds of experience; but no such result can be derived for primary quality concepts. In consequence, the mind of a being capable of thoughts concerning secondary qualities will, because of this necessary connexion with experience, pose a problem for physicalism not posed by a mind capable of thoughts concerning primary qualities: in this respect thoughts about colour are like thoughts about pain, and both are unlike thoughts about shape. And this implies that a thinking being whose thoughts are restricted to the absolute conception will not have the kind of problematic subjectivity Nagel isolates.[13]

Something similar seems to be true in the case of indexical thoughts. Earlier I associated indexical thought with direct conscious awareness, in particular with possession of a first-person perspective: deploying indexical concepts presupposes such direct awareness. But eternal thoughts—e.g., thoughts about arithmetic or the laws of physics—do not seem similarly bound up with direct conscious acquaintance with things in the world.[14] If this is so, then indexical thoughts

[12] So even if someone were to claim, on general empiricist grounds, that possession of the concept *square* requires experience of square things—as it might be claimed that possessing mathematical concepts requires experience of empirical states of affairs in which such concepts are satisfied—there would still be an asymmetry with the concept *red*, since experience enters the very analysis of that concept. (In fact it is hard to see how the general empiricist claim can be maintained if a concept is agreed not to be *inherently* sensory.)

[13] This is true only if such a being could possess the absolute conception of the world without having had experience of it. If this is not possible, then the claim should be reformulated to read: no concept possessed by this purely objective thinker constitutively requires the enjoyment of *specific* sensory experiences, and so involves a specific subjective state as its *sine qua non*.

[14] What it seems difficult to make room for in an objective physicalist account of reality is the existence of *perspectives* on the world, and this seems (as I have argued) bound up in direct cognitive awareness of things in the world. Nagel once tried to capture this uncapturability thesis by claiming that no amount of information expressed non-indexically could ever entail '*I* am C.M.', and he could have made a parallel point about the other indexicals: see his 'Physicalism', p. 109.

and eternal thoughts are asymmetrically related to a mental feature often supposed especially troubling for a physicalist view of the mind—namely, the feature of first-person conscious awareness. Thus the egocentric character of indexical thought makes it peculiarly subjective, in somewhat the way in which the experiential associations of thoughts about secondary qualities confer subjectivity upon them. (This is not, of course, to say that thoughts with purely objective content pose *no* problem for physicalism.)

At the level of experience, there seem to be two respects in which secondary quality mental content is more problematic than primary quality content—two respects in which looking red is more refractory to physicalist accounts than looking square. We cannot capture the difference by saying, as we did with respect to thoughts, that there is something it is like to have an experiential content of the former kind but not so for experiential content of the latter kind, since the two kinds of content are inseparable. There might be this asymmetry if purely primary quality experience were a real possibility; but since it is not there is, as a matter of necessity, always something it is subjectively like to see something square. But two other asymmetries can be discerned. The first is that the common tactic of transferring representational content onto the physical world cannot work for experience of secondary qualities: it might be plausible to suggest that an experience as of something square can be explained in terms of a relation to objective physical square things, but we cannot explain experience as of a red object in a parallel fashion.[15] The reason is simply that being red is not an objective physical property; experiential content in respect of this quality cannot therefore be transferred onto the world of

---

[15] Thus we might try to explain what it is for an experience to have a representational content as of something square by saying that the experience has the content it would have were the perceiver to be seeing something square; but if we try this for an experience as of something red we end up predicating 'red' of physical objects—and we know that this property has no place in the physicist's scheme of things: see U. T. Place, 'Is Consciousness a Brain Process?', p. 30, for such a view of ascriptions of experiential content.

physically comprehensible things. The content of such experience is, on the subjectivist view, contributed by the mind; so a physicalist has to account for this specific kind of representational content as well as the general phenomenon of perceptual awareness. It would be different if, with Armstrong, we believed that secondary qualities could be reduced to primary quality bases in the object, for then the objectivising tactic would be as workable for this kind of mental content as for experience of primary qualities; but rejecting such reductionism leaves secondary qualities stubbornly in the mind. There is more in the cosmos that is irreducibly mental when secondary qualities are construed subjectively.[16]

The second problem relates to functionalist theories of experience. A well-known objection to functionalist analyses of experience issues from the claim that experience can vary in its content while preserving its causal role, as in inverted spectrum cases.[17] Now it is a notable fact that such familiar cases of content inversion always involve secondary qualities: it is not supposed plausible that two experiences could be functionally isomorphic though differing in that one was an experience as of a square object and the other an experience as of a round object, but it is natural to suppose that inversions of red and green are compatible with functional isomorphism. Behavioural dispositions seem (necessarily) sensitive to variations in primary quality experiential content, but there is not this kind of sensitivity for secondary quality content. This *prima facie* asymmetry accordingly entails a difference in the susceptibility of the two kinds of

---

[16] A vivid way to put the point is this: suppose we had a complete description of the world before there were any perceivers, including the micro-properties of physical objects; this description would omit all mention of colours, tastes, sounds, and so forth. When we add conscious perceivers we add all these sensory qualities, in addition to the states of perceiving them: so a physicalist needs to account for more than just the perceptual states—there are also the apparently non-physical *qualities* onto which these states are directed.

[17] A classic statement of this problem can be found in Schlick, 'Form and Content'. See also Block, 'Troubles with Functionalism', and Shoemaker, 'Functionalism and Qualia'.

experiential feature to functionalist (and hence physicalist) analysis. Again, this should not be taken to mean that there is a possible kind of perceptual experience which does not present the problem of content inversion, a kind for which functionalism goes through; for the inseparability thesis ensures that if there is this problem for secondary quality experience, then the problem arises for *any* conceivable kind of perceiver.[18]

Let us agree that the two kinds of content differ in respect of functional definability, at least *prima facie*: we can then ask what explains the difference. This is worth asking because we might discover some *principled* reason for the non-functional character of sensory experience.[19] A sketch of the explanation is as follows: which secondary qualities a creature perceives depends upon its own subjective contribution to the content of its experience, whereas primary qualities are perceived because they are objectively out there; and this difference imposes different requirements on the creature's behaviour. Primary quality experience represents objects as having properties which determine their causal powers; so correctness in how the primary qualities of a thing are perceptually represented is critical to whether the movements of the body informed by those experiences will interact satisfactorily with the object of perception. If something looks square, then the perceiver's body will, inasmuch as it is informed by that experience, move in a manner suited to square things; but if the object is not in point of fact square,

---

[18] This is on the assumption that, for any possible sense, there will exist a permutation of the secondary qualities perceived by that sense which preserves functional role: that is, any sense has some analogue of red–green inversion. I do not know how to prove this claim, but it seems to me quite plausible—mainly because I think it cannot be just an *accident* that our actual senses give rise to such possibilities.

[19] That is, we might come up with something that made it seem not merely *unlucky* that experience poses this problem for functionalism; we might find some feature of experience which made the problem predictable. (It does not seem that the fact that there is something it is like to enjoy sensory experience by itself explains the logical possibility of content inversion.) Furthermore, the discovery of a rationale for the claimed independence of experiential content from functional role might help us determine with greater surety whether this independence claim is really in the end correct.

the movement will be inappropriate. So behaviour is sensitive to primary quality content because error in how things are thus represented has repercussions with respect to the interactions of the perceiver's body and the object of perception: it is the objectivity of primary qualities which guarantees behavioural sensitivity to primary quality experience. But this is not so for secondary qualities: since they have no causal powers any perceptual misrepresentation of them would not have the untoward consequences in respect of bodily interaction which we saw to ensue in the case of primary qualities.[20] So three things go together: the idea that differences of secondary quality perception do not entail error; the causal irrelevance of secondary qualities; and the (possible) insensitivity of functional description to secondary quality variation. They go together because we do not, in the case of secondary qualities, have the idea that correctness in how things are perceived is critical to the suitability of one's behaviour in causal interaction with the object of perception. In short, it is precisely the subjectivity of secondary qualities which explains the functional indefinability of secondary quality experience; behaviour does not need to be sensitive to qualities whose instantiation is determined by the subjective contribution of the mind. If this is the right diagnosis of why secondary quality experience is not functionally definable, then (given the inseparability thesis) the problem sensory experience poses for functionalism begins to look principled and fundamental: it arises from the fact that the perceiving mind necessarily makes a subjective contribution to the content of experience. The point here is not (or not just) that secondary quality experience is subjective in the sense that there is something it is like to have it, for this applies equally to primary quality experiential content; what

[20] Bennett seems to me to be making a closely related point about the difference in this respect between primary and secondary qualities in his discussion of 'size-blindness' and 'colour-blindness': *Locke, Berkeley, Hume*, pp. 96 ff. My suggestion is that *this* difference explains why experiential content in respect of the two kinds of quality is differentially susceptible of functional characterisation.

generates the functional uncapturability of sensory experience is the fact that secondary qualities are subjective in the further sense that they are *contributed* by the mind—this along with the inseparability thesis.

The point I have just been making about the functional asymmetry between primary quality and secondary quality experience should be distinguished from the contention, discussed by Schlick, that experience has both a form and a content, and that the content may vary though the form stays fixed.[21] Schlick is interested in the question of the communicability of the character of experience, and hence in whether a perceiver's behavioural dispositions can exhaustively reveal what sort of experience is being enjoyed. He accordingly considers cases of inversions of secondary quality experience (though he does not note that the 'content' he considers relates specifically to secondary qualities), concluding that it is possible for the *form* of experience to show up in behaviour but that the content seems ineffable. The general position here mirrors the asymmetry between primary and secondary quality experience, but it would be wrong to take the *form* of experience to consist in the perception of some primary quality: for Schlick's distinction applies *within* the realm of secondary quality experience—he is discussing the formal relations between (say) colour qualities, not some primary quality of objects which is given simultaneously with the perception of colour. This difference between our distinction and Schlick's means that the explanation offered above of the former distinction does not carry over to the latter distinction: we cannot, it seems, appeal to the objective possession by objects of causally

---

[21] Schlick, op. cit.; also Harrison, *Form and Content*. These authors are principally concerned with content inversion as a problem for our knowledge of other minds, a problem which is obviously intimately connected with the problem raised for functionalism. If what I have said about primary quality experience is right, then our knowledge of how someone perceives the world in respect of its primary qualities does not present the *same* problem—rather as Schlick thinks that the *structure* of someone's experience is perfectly verifiable and hence knowable by another. (I am not saying that I believe these alleged epistemological problems to be insuperable.)

efficacious properties corresponding to the form of subjective experience; so differences in the form of two perceivers' experiences of the world would not have the sorts of untoward consequences mentioned before. If the form of experience did determine a unique functional description, as Schlick in effect claims, this would not then have the same rationale as the sensitivity of functional description to primary quality experiential content; though the potential variation of secondary quality content would have the same explanation in the two cases. But Schlick's considerations do (if they are taken seriously) suggest another way in which secondary quality experience seems to elude a purely objectivist account of the mind: that we can make the distinction of form and content at all shows the peculiar nature of subjective experiential representations—their (apparent) proneness to float free of objective physical facts. It is not that I want to assert dogmatically that experience does in this way float free of the physical—perhaps there is some deep conceptual problem about the possibility of content inversion; I am merely noting certain intuitive distinctions that our mental concepts seem to invite us to make and remarking upon their apparent consequences.[22]

(iii) *Values and secondary qualities.* Hume wrote of moral value:

It lies in yourself, not in the object. So that when you pronounce any action or character to be vicious, you mean nothing, but that from the constitution of your nature you have a feeling or sentiment of blame from the contemplation of it. Vice and virtue, therefore, may be compared to sounds, colours, heat and cold, which, according to modern philosophy, are not qualities in objects, but perceptions in the mind: And this discovery in morals, like that other in physics, is to be regarded as a considerable advancement of the speculative sciences; though, like that too, it has little or no influence in practice.[23]

[22] In general in this section my aim has not been to argue that physicalism is false; on the contrary, I believe it to be true (or at least a certain version of it: see my 'Philosophical Materialism'). I have wished only to bring out some of the problems physicalists must face up to concerning secondary qualities if they are to sustain their convictions.

[23] Hume, *Treatise of Human Nature*, Bk III, Pt i, sec. i, p. 469.

The comparison of which Hume speaks has also been proposed by more recent writers (Harman,[24] Mackie,[25] Wiggins[26]). Obviously the aptness of the comparison depends (a) upon one's conception of secondary qualities, and (b) upon the view of moral values one wishes to endorse; and it is notable that different writers use the comparison to advance quite different views of ethics, depending upon the conception of secondary qualities they presuppose.[27] I do not think, however, that anyone who proposes the comparison wishes to presuppose a thoroughly objectivist conception, of the kind suggested by Armstrong and by Kripke.[28] That would be inadvisable for two reasons (aside from the incorrectness of that conception): first, because the idea of a reductive theoretical identification of value properties with some underlying empirical real essence seems plainly absurd; and second, because the comparison could, if that were the presupposed view of secondary qualities, equally well have been made with other natural kind concepts. The presupposed view tends rather to be something like the Lockean conception, variously articulated.[29] I shall argue that *if* this is the presupposed view, then the resulting ethical theory has consequences we do well to resist; on any reasonably sane

[24] Harman, *The Nature of Morality*, pp. 44 ff. Harman is expounding rather than endorsing the comparison in this passage.

[25] Mackie, *Ethics*, pp. 19-20, and *Hume's Moral Theory*, p. 136.

[26] Wiggins, 'Truth, Invention, and the Meaning of Life', pp. 348-9.

[27] Harman in fact favours a form of moral relativism, and seems to say that relativism is not true of secondary qualities such as colour (op. cit., p. 45), though he appears to admit their dispositionality. Mackie holds an 'error theory' of secondary qualities and employs the analogy to promote a parallel theory of moral evaluation—like Hume he thinks that we mistakenly objectify moral properties: see his *Ethics*, chap. 1. Wiggins appeals to the comparison in order to demonstrate the consistency of the thesis that values have 'objectivity' and 'externality' as well as 'anthropocentricity': op. cit., p. 349.

[28] See Armstrong, *A Materialist Theory of the Mind*, chap. 12; Kripke, *Naming and Necessity*, p. 140, note 71.

[29] That is, the authors cited do seem to hold that the psychological states of colour experiences and moral attitudes enter the *analysis* of the corresponding predicates of objects; they do not serve merely to fix the reference of these predicates. But these authors do not spell out their view of secondary qualities in sufficient detail to determine whether they would agree with the characterisation I have adopted in this work—and which I shall direct against them.

view of ethics the comparison with secondary qualities is unapt. Perhaps the writers who have endorsed the comparison have not really wished moral values to have all the salient features of secondary qualities, intending the comparison to be more tenuous than Hume himself recommends; if so, my remarks will serve to underline the limits of the comparison. Let us begin by spelling the analogy out a bit.

The dispositional thesis about colour says that being red consists in looking red to some perceiver(s). A parallel dispositional thesis about value properties will hold that (e.g.) being good consists in a propensity on the part of good things to elicit in observers reactions of moral approval: 'good' applies to something if and only if it produces 'sentiments of approbation' in people. Thus, just as secondary quality predicates have sensory states as part of their satisfaction conditions, so moral predicates have certain affective or valuational psychological states as part of their satisfaction conditions: any account of what it is for an object to have a moral property will therefore make essential reference to certain psychological reactions in appropriately constituted beings. This account of values seems to jibe with certain putative features of moral properties which it may be thought desirable to capture. First, the analogy allows us to say that moral properties are literally *perceptible* features of the external world, even though they are analysed in terms of psychological reactions, since secondary qualities combine these two characteristics.[30] It is true that Hume himself wanted to promote a more introspectionist account of moral sense, and took secondary quality experience to provide a model for this; but once we reject the idea that subjectivism about secondary qualities implies their instantiation by mental items and not by external objects, we can agree with Hume about the analogy while disagreeing about its

---

[30] Thus this aspect of the analogy would, I think, be welcomed by McDowell, in view of his thesis that moral properties are detectable by the exercise of a *perceptual* capacity: see his 'Are Moral Requirements Hypothetical Imperatives?', p. 23.

consequences for the character of the faculty of moral sense —no mistake of objectification need be admitted in either case.[31] This means that we can quite properly regard values as 'in the world' despite their involvement with the psychological: moral predicates are quite correctly and literally applicable to external objects—it is just that their being so constitutively involves a relation to the reactions of moral evaluators. Second, the manifest causal irrelevance of moral properties finds an analogy in secondary qualities: value predicates do not feature in the explanatory theories of physical science because the moral properties of things do not contribute to their causal powers—and the same is true of secondary qualities.[32] Moreover, the analogy suggests an explanation in the value case: moral properties belong to objects only in virtue of their relations to observers' mental states, and such relations contribute nothing to the intrinsic causal powers of objects. And if it is asked *why* we apprehend the world as containing such theoretically otiose properties, we can give parallel answers in the two cases: we perceive the moral properties and secondary qualities we do, not because of their role in a theory of how the world works, but to aid us practically in 'the conduct of life'.[33] Third, we have an analogue of the point that the content of (say) colour experience requires to be specified by using the colour concept the experience is invoked to 'define'; for the moral reactions elicited in people likewise have an intentional content which invites specification in terms of moral concepts.

[31] This would be a case in which the mind 'spreads itself on the world' but not in such a way as to commit any error: we should not move from 'ϕ would not be ascribable to things in the world unless there were conscious beings with certain psychological reactions' to 'the mind is in error in taking ϕ to be a property of things in the world'. To justify this move it would have additionally to be shown that 'common sense' regards moral properties as non-dispositional *absolute* properties of objects.

[32] The analogy thus helps us resist the idea that moral properties must be pseudo-properties because their instantiation makes no difference to how the world works; for this is also true of secondary qualities yet they are clearly real properties of things.

[33] This seems to be Locke's view of both sorts of property: *Essay* Bk IV, esp. xii, 11.

Thus a reaction of moral approval is precisely a judgement (or perhaps feeling) to the effect that a presented state of affairs is *good*; moral 'experiences' have intentional content, and this consists precisely in representing the world as having certain moral properties. This feature of the dispositional analysis of value is somewhat obscured in Hume's own development of it, because he is apt to gloss 'sentiments of approbation/disapprobation' in terms of sensations of pleasure or pain, which presumably do not have the sort of intentional content which gives rise to this third analogy with secondary qualities. But, first, it is not to be supposed that Hume adopts this view of the relevant moral reactions out of a desire to escape a charge of circularity of the kind sometimes levelled at the dispositional analysis of secondary qualities; and, second, this sensational interpretation of moral reactions is clearly, if taken literally, hopeless as an account of what the defining moral reactions consist in——for I can obviously morally approve of a state of affairs which gives me a head-ache. Any reasonable version of the dispositional analysis of values will, then, find itself employing moral concepts in the specification of the moral reactions concerned. This of course precludes any claim of strict definition, as it did in the case of secondary qualities, but a thesis of logical equivalence can still be formulated, as well as the contention that moral facts just 'consist in' dispositions to produce such reactions.[34] (The evident reasonableness and internal coherence of this position should help allay doubts about the parallel position with respect to secondary qualities.) So far, then, the analogy between values and secondary qualities seems to be holding up; but I think there are two further consequences of the comparison which destroy its viability——and these spring directly from the subjectivism which accompanies the dispositional thesis.

[34] Comparably with the case of secondary qualities, we can formulate this as the claim that things are good because we judge them to be good, rather than that we judge them to be good because they are (independently) good; or again, that things count as good *in virtue of* their being judged good. No claim of *semantic* priority is entailed by these formulations.

The two consequences concern moral epistemology and
the nature of moral truth; they are really two aspects of the
same point. The problem for moral epistemology which arises
from construing values on the model of secondary qualities is
that the notion of moral *error* becomes problematic: it
becomes hard to see how the moral judgements of a person
or community could be mistaken. We saw in chapters 2 and
4 that there is a sense in which a perceiver (or group of
perceivers) cannot be in error about which secondary qualities
the world contains, since the standard of correctness for
secondary quality ascriptions is set by the phenomenological
character of perceptual experience—and this is infallibly
given. Hume was perspicacious enough to see that an analogous consequence held under his dispositional theory of
moral value: 'the distinction of moral good and evil is founded
on the pleasure or pain, which results from the view of any
sentiment, or character; and as that pleasure or pain cannot
be unknown to the person who feels it, it follows, that there
is just so much vice or virtue in any character, as everyone
places in it, and that it is impossible in this particular that we
can ever be mistaken.'[35] Hume thinks to find confirmation of
this epistemological consequence in the reliability of the
moral judgements of the ordinary man; but in fact his theory
makes it very difficult to see how *any* genuine moral mistake
is possible, since moral correctness just consists in the
occurrence of appropriate mental states on the part of the
judger.[36] It might be supposed that room for moral error can
be made under the analogy by noting that our practice of
(say) colour ascription acknowledges a distinction between
real and apparent colour. But once the foundation and
character of that distinction are clearly grasped it should be

---

[35] Hume, *Treatise*, Bk III, Pt ii, sec. viii, pp. 546–7.

[36] See Hume, ibid., p. 546, for the assertion of moral infallibility. It does
not seem that a Humean could escape this consequence by appealing (*contra*
Hume himself) to an alleged fallibility in our introspective reports: for even if
these were fallible, this source hardly adds up to the kind of moral error we regard
as possible; and we do want to allow that a person could be perfectly right as to
the character of his moral reaction to a situation and yet be mistaken in his moral
reaction.

obvious that it does not supply what we require; for the distinction rests upon a consensus *within* the realm of perceptual experience—there is no reaction-independent criterion of correctness for such ascriptions. This point shows that moral error, on the dispositional theory, could consist at most in a failure of conformity of one person's moral reactions with the reactions of others: the theory cannot allow that a whole community might be in moral error, or that a solitary judger might make moral mistakes, since this would require some standard of correctness external to that provided by an essentially arbitrary norm of moral reaction.[37] If the standard were to change, as it could for secondary qualities, then moral judgements would cease to be true which once counted as instances of moral knowledge—we could not say that the change of moral reaction constituted any kind of moral mistake.[38]

It might be suggested that the dispositional theory could allow for moral nescience by invoking an analogy with colour-blindness; for this phenomenon certainly counts as a *deficiency* in colour perception, and its existence is quite compatible with treating colours as dispositional. The deficiency of the colour-blind is basically a matter of making fewer or coarser colour discriminations than those made by normal perceivers; so the suggestion will be that the dispositional theory of value can similarly acknowledge the possibility that one person's moral reactions be more discriminating than those of others. But a moment's thought shows that this kind of deficiency does not add up to what we intuitively think of as moral error: superiority of moral

[37] That is, we find the thought of morally evaluating the 'normal' moral reactions in our community not to be incoherent, whereas it *would* be incoherent to press the question whether the colour perceptions of normal observers in normal conditions are themselves veridical. The notion of 'normality' here invoked is a basically statistical notion, but we do not likewise think that what *most* people in our community regard as good sets the standard for what *is* good.

[38] Suppose I want to do something I know to be morally wrong: I could, according to the analogy with secondary qualities, set out to still my conscience by contriving a state of affairs in which people in my community come to approve of the action in question, thus altering (by propaganda or brain surgery) the standards of moral truth!

judgement does not consist solely (if it consists at all) in the ability merely to make *more* discriminations than others; it consists in being *right* in one's judgements about particular cases. Two people could in principle be capable of making equally fine-grained moral distinctions, and yet one of them be right and the other wrong with respect to a case which they can both equally discriminate from other cases. Moral blindness is not (or is not principally) a matter of perceiving two situations as indistinguishable in value which others perceive as having different values; it consists rather in assigning the *wrong* value to a situation which the judger can morally distinguish from other situations as well as the next man.[39] To see this, consider a moral analogue to the case of human and Martian colour perception: the moral ascriptions of the two communities are equally complex and fine-grained, but different values are assigned to the same state of affairs. In the colour case we should say that no error is involved on either side; and this is predicted by the dispositional theory. But in the moral case the analogous prediction is not borne out: we want to say that one side (at least) must be morally wrong. In the case of ethics, on our customary understanding of it, it makes sense to entertain the notion of an ideal moral being, one whose moral reactions may well be superior to our own; this is a way of giving content to the thought that we might be morally mistaken about a matter, and it gives shape to the idea of moral progress. But the notion of an ideal perceiver of secondary qualities—one whose experience better reveals the *real* colours and tastes of things—this is not a coherent notion. Perhaps the idea

---

[39] Harman seems to suggest that the phenomenon of colour-blindness shows that relativism about colour ascriptions is not true, and that an analogous notion of moral blindness might similarly ensure a non-relativistic conception of moral ascriptions: op. cit., pp. 45–6. In addition to the point made in the text, I observe, against this, that it is often proper to criticise someone on moral grounds for making *too many* moral distinctions—for making moral distinctions where there are no moral differences: but it would be senseless to criticise someone's colour perception on the ground that his visual system divides the spectrum into more colours than ours does, since the making of (systematic) colour distinctions is *constitutive* of there being corresponding colour differences.

of a superior moral point of view, and the correlative idea that our moral beliefs are fallible, does not extend so far as the idea of an ideal scientific point of view; but it certainly seems to extend further than the analogy with secondary qualities is equipped to permit.

The point I have just made obviously depends upon acceptance of some kind of 'moral realism', i.e. the (modest) thesis that moral reality might not be just as we suppose it; my next point assumes that extreme moral relativism is not to be entertained.[40] This point is really just a development of the last one: if moral truth consists in facts about moral reactions, as the comparison with secondary qualities alleges, then clearly differences of moral reaction will give rise to a relativity in moral truth; moral difference will not be interpretable as moral disagreement. I do not think that this degree of relativism was contemplated or intended by the writers who have endorsed the comparison, but anyway it follows pretty directly from the dispositional theory. Someone might reply that the impact of the threatened relativism is reduced by constitutional limitations upon the kinds of moral reactions open to human beings: it is contrary to human nature, the reply may go, to suppose that human beings might differ in their moral reactions in the radical way in which Martians might differ from us in their colour perception. Two points should be made: first, we should be careful not to let our sense of these limitations be informed by a tacitly objectivist account of value—as we would when imagining perceptual variation in respect of primary qualities; and second, the logical point survives conceding such limitations upon the variability of human reactions—for surely there are *possible* beings whose moral reactions differ radically from our own.[41] Since value concepts are being *analysed* in

---

[40] Of course someone of nihilistic or revisionary moral tendencies might invoke the analogy with secondary qualities expressly to undermine our customary conception of morality. I am not claiming to refute such a nihilist; I am asking how much of morality *as we have it* is captured by the analogy.

[41] I can imagine a position in which this latter claim is denied: it might be maintained that any conceivable moral being must have a specific moral

terms of dispositions to produce moral reactions, the mere logical possibility of radically different reactions introduces an inevitable relativism into the satisfaction conditions of value concepts; so no adventitious limitations upon human reactions can lessen the conceptual consequences of taking the dispositional theory seriously.

To reject the analogy with secondary qualities is not, of course, to accept an analogy with primary qualities; and indeed such an analogy would immediately attract forceful objections, notably that moral properties do not have the role in causal-explanatory theories which is characteristic of primary qualities. Neither analogy seems to me appropriate. In *some* respects values are, I think, better compared to mathematical or modal properties, these combining a certain objectivity with transcendence of the empirical causal order: but this is not the place to enter into a full-scale positive discussion of the metaphysics of moral value.

Let me finally observe that there is no real analogue of the inseparability thesis in respect of the perception of moral value. For we can readily conceive of perceivers who do not perceive the world as containing moral properties: animals are presumably in this case. Awareness of values, unlike

psychology as a matter of necessity. Thus it might be denied that it is, for example, conceptually possible for a moral being to judge that pointless suffering is a great good: such a moral psychology just cannot be made sense of. I do not wish to dispute that, at some basic level of moral reaction, such a position may be correct —as it would be plainly *in*correct to make an analogous claim about the necessity for any visual perceiver to have the specific kinds of colour experience we have. But I do not think this admission can lessen the force of the criticism I make in the text. First, there is the question of those aspects of moral psychology which do admit of variation: are we to say that the corresponding moral judgements have their truth-value fixed by these variable moral reactions? Second, the position being advanced does not prohibit us from formulating our question by means of a counterfactual with an impossible antecedent: we can still ask 'if (*per impossibile*) there were a moral being with a moral psychology totally different from ours, would we want to allow that the moral judgements of such a being, though they strike us as morally indefensible, may nevertheless be true relatively to that being?' I think that, confronted with such an impossible moral being, we would think it entirely proper to voice our moral disagreement in the strongest possible terms. The point is that defining moral truth in terms of moral reactions is unacceptably relativist even when the implicit relativism *cannot* show itself as moral difference.

awareness of secondary qualities, is not constitutive of what it is to have perceptual experience of the external world. This is not, of course, to say that perception of the non-moral properties of things is possible in the absence of perception of their moral properties *if* the perceiver is equipped with moral sense: it may be, for all I have said, that the moral sense, once it is possessed, is always brought into operation when the world is perceived. But this does not restore the analogy with secondary qualities, since an ability to perceive them must be present in any being with the ability to perceive at all; and this is what is false of moral sense. However, though there is no inseparability thesis linking moral awareness with the existence of sense-perception, there may yet be (I think there is) a true inseparability thesis applicable at the level of *thought*—the thesis, namely, that moral awareness is necessarily implicated in the possession of *rationality*.[42] But this locates the apprehension of moral value more in the intellectual faculties than in the strictly sensory— where I myself would prefer to locate it anyway.[43]

[42] I take this to be roughly Kant's doctrine: see his *Foundations of the Metaphysics of Morals.*
[43] Nagel emphasises the connexion between the moral faculty and the faculty of reason in *The Possibility of Altruism.*

9
Summary Conclusion

At the beginning of this essay I undertook to distinguish between certain objective and subjective aspects of our ways of representing the world, to articulate the distinctive characteristics of the two aspects, and to say how they are related. I suggested that perception of secondary qualities and indexical thought counted as subjective modes of representation, in contrast to the objective character of primary quality perception and non-indexical thought. These two exemplifications of the subjective view were claimed to exhibit certain quasi-logical laws governing the internal relations between the ways in which the world is subjectively represented: these laws have their source in the constitution of the subject. I also said that the identification of these subjective features enjoys a certain kind of incorrigibility, and that they operate as a sort of grid laid over the world by the representing mind. I then urged that these two kinds of subjective representation are ineliminable from any mind capable of perceptual and direct awareness of the world, and I tried to offer some sort of explanation of this inelimin-ability—noting the *prima facie* need for such an explana-tion and the difficulty of supplying one. I concluded that a Kantian-sounding position was encouraged by the results obtained hitherto, though no noumenal world was called for. With the nature and status of the subjective view thus clarified, I went on to consider how an objective and absolute conception of the world relates to the world as subjectively presented, arguing that the two styles of representation are compatible, though essentially different in their intrinsic character. I ended with some remarks about three issues in which secondary qualities have played a part, applying my earlier conclusions to the questions raised. Throughout I tried to illuminate the topics dealt with by exploiting certain analogies between secondary qualities and indexicals. Many of the questions I raised were old (and some of them may have seemed odd), but I hope their persistent interest emerged, as well as their difficulty. If I did not succeed in giving convincing answers to all the questions raised, I trust that the topic of primary and secondary qualities and that of indexical thought were seen to have a wider significance than has often been recognised.[1]

---

[1] I do not mean to imply that I am alone in recognising this wider significance.

Bibliography

Anscombe, G. E. M. 'The First Person'. In *Mind and Language*, ed. S. Guttenplan. Oxford: Clarendon Press, 1975.

Armstrong, D. M. *A Materialist Theory of the Mind*. London: Routledge, 1968.

— 'Perception, Sense Data and Causality'. In *Perception and Identity*, ed. G. F. Macdonald. London: Macmillan, 1979.

Ayers, M. R. 'The Theory of Perception'. Chapter Two of a forthcoming book on Locke, to be published by Routledge.

Bennett, J. F. *Locke, Berkeley, Hume: Central Themes*. Oxford: Clarendon Press, 1971.

Berkeley, G. *The Principles of Human Knowledge*, ed. G. J. Warnock. London: Fontana, 1962.

— *A New Theory of Vision*. London: Everyman, 1960.

Block, N. 'Troubles with Functionalism'. In *Readings in Philosophy of Psychology*, vol. I, ed. N. Block. Cambridge, Mass.: Harvard University Press, 1980.

Bradley, F. H. *Appearance and Reality*. Oxford: Clarendon Press, 1897.

Burge, T. 'Other Bodies'. In *Thought and Object*, ed. A. Woodfield. Oxford: Clarendon Press, 1982.

Campbell, K. 'Colours'. In *Contemporary Philosophy in Australia*, ed. R. Brown and C. D. Rollins. London: George Allen and Unwin, 1969.

Castañeda, H.-N. *Thinking and Doing*. Dordrecht: Reidel, 1975.

Chisholm, R. *The First Person*. Sussex: Harvester, 1981.

Descartes, R. *Meditations*. In *Philosophical Works of Descartes*, vol. I, eds. E. S. Haldane and G. R. T. Ross. Cambridge: Cambridge University Press, 1967.

Dummett, M. A. E. 'What is a Theory of Meaning? (II)'. In *Truth and Meaning*, eds. G. Evans and J. McDowell. Oxford: Clarendon Press, 1976.

— 'Common Sense and Physics'. In *Perception and Identity*, ed. G. F. Macdonald. London: Macmillan, 1979.

— *The Interpretation of Frege's Philosophy*. London: Duckworth, 1982.

Eddington, A. S. *The Nature of the Physical World*. Cambridge: Cambridge University Press, 1928.

Evans, G. 'Things Without the Mind: a Commentary on Chapter 2 of Strawson's *Individuals*'. in *Philosophical Subjects*, ed. Z. van Straaten. Oxford: Oxford University Press, 1980.

— 'Understanding Demonstratives'. In *Meaning and Understanding*, eds. H. Paret and J. Bouvresse. New York: De Gruyter, 1981.

Frege, G. 'On Sense and Reference'. In *Philosophical Writings*, eds. P. Geach and M. Black. Oxford: Blackwell, 1966.

— 'The Thought: a Logical Inquiry'. In *Philosophical Logic*, ed. P. F. Strawson. Oxford: Oxford University Press, 1967.

Geach, P. T. *Mental Acts*. London: Routledge, 1957.

Grice, H. P. 'Meaning'. *Philosophical Review* 66, 1957.

— 'The Causal Theory of Perception'. *Proceedings of the Aristotelian Society*, Supp. Vol. 35, 1961.

Harman, G. *The Nature of Morality*. Oxford: Oxford University Press, 1977.

Harrison, B. *Form and Content*. Oxford: Blackwell, 1973.

Hooker, C. 'An Evolutionary Naturalist Realist Doctrine of Perception and Secondary Qualities. In *Perception and Cognition: Issues in the Foundations of Psychology*, ed. W. Savage. Minnesota: University of Minnesota Press, 1978.

Hume, D. *A Treatise of Human Nature*, ed. L. A. Selby-Bigge. Oxford: Oxford University Press, 1960.

Husserl, E. *Logical Investigations*. London: Routledge, 1970.

— *Ideas, General Introduction to Pure Phenomenology*. London: Allen and Unwin, 1958.

Jackson, F. *Perception*. Cambridge: Cambridge University Press, 1977.

Jackson, R. 'Locke's Distinction between Primary and Secondary Qualities'. *Mind* 38, 1929.

Kant, I. *Critique of Pure Reason*, trans. N. Kemp Smith. London: Macmillan, 1933.

— *Prolegomena to any Future Metaphysics*, ed. L. W. Beck. New York: Liberal Arts, 1950.

— *Foundations of the Metaphysics of Morals*, ed. L. W. Beck. New York: Liberal Arts, 1959.

Kaplan, D. *Demonstratives*. Unpublished, 1977.

— 'On the Logic of Demonstratives'. In *Contemporary Perspectives in the Philosophy of Language*, eds. P. French, *et al.* Morris: University of Minnesota Press, 1979.

Kneale, W. C. 'Sensation and the Physical World'. *Philosophical Quarterly*, January 1951.

Kripke, S. *Naming and Necessity*. Oxford: Blackwell, 1980.

Lewis, D. 'Attitudes *De Dicto* and *De Se*'. *Philosophical Review* 87, 1979.

Locke, J. *An Essay Concerning Human Understanding*, ed. A. D. Woozley. London: Fontana, 1964.

Mackie, J. L. *Problems from Locke*. Oxford: Oxford University Press, 1976.

— *Ethics: Inventing Right and Wrong*. Penguin Books, 1977.

— *Hume's Moral Theory*. London: Routledge, 1980.

McDowell, J. H. 'Are Moral Requirements Hypothetical Imperatives?'. *Proceedings of the Aristotelian Society*, Supp. Vol., 1978.

McGinn, C. 'Mental States, Natural Kinds and Psychophysical Laws'. *Proceedings of the Aristotelian Society*, Supp. Vol., 1978.

— 'Philosophical Materialism'. *Synthese* 44, June 1980.

— 'Functionalism and Phenomenalism: a Critical Note'. *Australasian Journal of Philosophy* 58, March 1980.

— 'The Structure of Content'. In *Thought and Object*, ed. A. Woodfield. Oxford: Clarendon Press, 1982.

Nagel, T. *The Possibility of Altruism.* Oxford: Clarendon Press, 1970.

— 'Physicalism'. *Philosophical Review* 74, 1965.

— 'Brain Bisection and the Unity of Consciousness'. In *Mortal Questions*. Cambridge: Cambridge University Press, 1979.

— 'What is it Like to be a Bat?' Also in *Mortal Questions*.

— 'Subjective and Objective'. Also in *Mortal Questions*.

Perry, J. 'Frege on Demonstratives'. *Philosophical Review* 86, 1977.

— 'The Problem of the Essential Indexical'. *Noûs* 13, 1979.

Pitcher, G. *A Theory of Perception.* Princeton: Princeton University Press, 1971.

Place, U. T. 'Is Consciousness a Brain Process?' In *The Philosophy of Mind*, ed. V. C. Chappell. Englewood Cliffs, N.J.: Prentice-Hall, 1962.

Putnam, H. 'The Nature of Mental States'. In *Mind, Language and Reality*. Cambridge: Cambridge University Press, 1975.

— 'The Meaning of "Meaning" '. Also in *Mind, Language and Reality*.

— *Reason, Truth and History*. Cambridge: Cambridge University Press, 1981.

Reid, T. *Essays on the Intellectual Powers of Man.* Cambridge, Mass.: MIT Press, 1969.

Russell, B. *The Problems of Philosophy.* Oxford: Oxford University Press, 1968.

— 'Sense Data and Physics'. In *Mysticism and Logic*. London: George Allen and Unwin, 1917.

— *An Inquiry Into Meaning and Truth*. Harmondsworth: Penguin Books, 1962.

— *Human Knowledge: its Scope and Limits.* London: George Allen and Unwin, 1948.

Schlick, M. 'Form and Content: an Introduction to Philosophical Thinking'. In *Philosophical Papers*, eds. H. Mulder and B. van de Velde-Schlick. Dordrecht: Reidel, 1979.

Sellars, W. 'Philosophy and the Scientific Image of Man'. In *Science, Perception and Reality*. London: Routledge, 1963.

Shoemaker, S. 'Self-Reference and Self-Awareness'. *Journal of Philosophy* 65, October 1968.

Shoemaker, S. 'Functionalism and Qualia'. *Philosophical Studies* 27, 1975.

Smart, J. J. C. *Philosophy and Scientific Realism.* London: Routledge, 1963.

Strawson, P. F. *Individuals.* London: Methuen, 1959.

— *The Bounds of Sense.* London: Methuen, 1966.

— 'Perception and its Objects'. In *Perception and Identity*, ed. G. F. Macdonald. London: Macmillan, 1979.

Wallace, J. 'Positive, Comparative, Superlative'. *Journal of Philosophy* 69, 1972.

Wiggins, D. 'Truth, Invention, and the Meaning of Life'. *British Academy Lecture*, 1976.

Williams, B. *Descartes: The Project of Pure Enquiry.* Harmondsworth: Penguin Books, 1978.

— 'Another Time, Another Place, Another Person'. In *Perception and Identity*, ed. G. F. Macdonald. London: Macmillan, 1979.

Wittgenstein, L. *Tractatus Logico-Philosophicus*, trans. D. F. Pears and B. F. McGuinness. London: Routledge, 1961.

— *The Blue and Brown Books.* Oxford: Blackwell, 1958.

— *Philosophical Investigations,* trans. G. E. M. Anscombe. Oxford: Blackwell, 1958.

— *Zettel*, trans. G. E. M. Anscombe. Oxford: Blackwell, 1967.

— *Remarks on Colour*, ed. G. E. M. Anscombe. Oxford: Blackwell, 1977.

Index